GW01337321

Barrie Mahoney worked as a teacher and head teacher in the south west of England, and then became a school inspector in England and Wales. A new life and career as a newspaper reporter in Spain's Costa Blanca led to him launching and editing an English language newspaper in the Canary Islands. Barrie's books include novels in 'The Prior's Hill Chronicles' series, as well as books for expats in the 'Letters from the Atlantic' series, which give an amusing and reflective view of life abroad.

Barrie writes regular columns for newspapers and magazines in Spain, Portugal, Ireland, Australia, South Africa, Canada, UK and the USA. He also designs mobile apps and websites to promote the Canary Islands and expat life, and is often asked to contribute to radio programmes about expat life.

Visit the author's websites:

http://barriemahoney.com
http://thecanaryislander.com

Other books by Barrie Mahoney

**Journeys & Jigsaws** (The Canary Islander Publishing) 2013
ISBN: 978-0957544475 (Paperback and eBook)

**Threads and Threats** (The Canary Islander Publishing) 2013
ISBN: 978-0992767105 (Paperback and eBook)

**Letters from the Atlantic** (The Canary Islander Publishing) 2013
ISBN: 978-0992767136 (Paperback and eBook)

**Living the Dream** (The Canary Islander Publishing) 2015
ISBN: 978-0992767198 (Paperback and eBook)

**Expat Survival** (The Canary Islander Publishing) 2015
ISBN: 978-0992767167 (Paperback and eBook)

**Message in a Bottle** (The Canary Islander Publishing) 2016
ISBN: 978-0995602700 (Paperback and eBook)

**Escape to the Sun** (The Canary Islander Publishing) 2016
ISBN: 978-0957544444 (Paperback and eBook)

**Expat Voice** (The Canary Islander Publishing) 2014
ISBN: 978-0992767174 (Paperback and eBook)

**Island in the Sun** (The Canary Islander Publishing) 2015
ISBN: 978-0992767181 (Paperback and eBook)

# Footprints in the Sand

## Barrie Mahoney

### The Canary Islander Publishing

© Copyright 2016

**Barrie Mahoney**

The right of Barrie Mahoney to be identified as author of this work has been asserted by him in accordance with the Copyright, Designs and Patents Act 1988.

**All Rights Reserved**

No reproduction, copy or transmission of this publication may be made without written permission. No paragraph of this publication may be reproduced, copied or transmitted save with the written permission of the author, or in accordance with the provisions of the Copyright Act 1956 (as amended).
Any person who commits any unauthorised act in relation to this publication may be liable to criminal prosecution and civil claims for damages.
A CIP catalogue record for this title is available from the British Library.

ISBN 978-0995602717
www.barriemahoney.com

First Published in 2016

**The Canary Islander Publishing**

## Acknowledgements

I would like to thank all those people that I have met on my journey to where I am now.

To supportive friends who helped me to overcome the many problems and frustrations that I faced and taught me much about learning to adapt to a new culture. Also, to friends in the UK, or scattered around the world, who have kept in touch despite being so far away.

To the people that I met whilst working as a newspaper reporter and editor in Spain and the Canary Islands, and for the privilege of sharing their successes and challenges in life.

## Disclaimer

This is a book about real people, real places and real events, but names of people and companies have been changed to avoid any embarrassment.

The Canary Islander

## Dedication

This book is dedicated to expats all over the world who dream of a new life, new experiences, new cultures, new opportunities to experience, taste and smell the excitement of a place that is of their own choosing and not merely based upon an accident of birth.

| **Contents** | 10 |
|---|---|
| | |
| **Preface** | 14 |
| | |
| **Footprints in the Sand** | 21 |
| The Sands of Time | 22 |
| Shifting Sand | 25 |
| An Escape to the Island of Los Lobos | 28 |
| Squirrelogy | 32 |
| | |
| **Coming or Going?** | 36 |
| The European Expat | 37 |
| Brexit – The Facts | 41 |
| Referendum? What Referendum? | 44 |
| Slipping into an Alternative Universe | 47 |
| Life Between the Devil and the Deep Blue Sea | 50 |
| Brexit is Good for Europe | 53 |
| Ever Been Bumped? | 56 |
| | |
| **Food and Drink** | 60 |
| The Long, Lazy Lunch | 61 |
| Black Tomatoes, Golden Kiwi and Red Bananas | 63 |
| Fuyu for You | 66 |
| The All-Inclusive Wrist Band | 69 |
| | |
| **Getting to Know You** | 72 |
| El Gordo – The Spanish Christmas Lottery | 73 |
| Making a Difference | 76 |
| The Domino Effect | 79 |

| | |
|---|---|
| A Winter's Tale | 81 |
| The Language Key | 84 |
| 'Por Favor' | 87 |
| | |
| **Fact, Fiction or What?** | 89 |
| Irish Monk Discovers New Canary Island, then loses it! | 90 |
| Atlantis or What? | 93 |
| Aliens Visit the Canary Islands | 96 |
| The Big Time Mix Up | 100 |
| Fuerteventura and the Nazis | 103 |
| Promises, Promises | 106 |
| | |
| **Keeping it Quirky** | 109 |
| The Story of the Smart Pole | 110 |
| It's the Wrong Kind of Sunshine! | 113 |
| The Booze Cruise | 115 |
| Living in Caves | 118 |
| Hug a Tree | 121 |
| Chinese Takeaway | 124 |
| | |
| **The Financial and Legal Expat** | 127 |
| A New Banking Experience for Expats | 128 |
| Holiday Health Insurance | 132 |
| Customs Confusion | 135 |
| No More UK Banking for Expats | 138 |
| Pineapple and Diamond Heists | 141 |
| The Insurance Fraud | 143 |
| Consumer Rights in Spain | 146 |
| Between a Rock and a Hard Place | 151 |
| | |
| **Living and Working Abroad** | 154 |
| The 'Would-be' Expat | 155 |

| | |
|---|---|
| Having a Ball | 158 |
| A New Expat Life or an Extended Holiday? | 161 |
| 'All-Inclusive' Poverty | 164 |
| Still Trying to Watch Brit TV in the Sun? | 167 |
| Healthcare for Expats in Spain – 'Convenio Especial' | 170 |
| Living in Spain – The Paperchase | 174 |
| Escape to the Ice | 178 |
| Getting Social | 181 |
| Back to School | 184 |

# Preface

## Preface

'Footprints in the Sand' is the eighth title in the 'Letters from the Atlantic' series. In some ways, this year has been the most difficult collection of 'Letters' to write, since much of the year has been focussed upon the Brexit debate. The decision whether or not to leave the European Union has for many expats been the most disturbing and disruptive period in their lives. At the time of writing, even though the Brexit dice has been thrown, exactly what that well-worn phrase used by the current Prime Minister, "Brexit means Brexit", means has yet to be established, leaving considerable uncertainty for many would-be, as well as current, expats living in Europe.

'Footprints in the Sand' is a reflection of the events that I have experienced over one year as an expat living in Spain and the Canary Islands; experiences that I hope will resonate with expats living all over the world. Thousands of expats have gone before us seeking new lives, experiences and adventures. All create footprints; some we choose to follow, whilst others we ignore. In time, footprints are washed away by new circumstances, opportunities and priorities. Nothing is forever and often we have to start again.

As many regular readers will already know, I am a committed European. I have never regarded myself as English, and feel uncomfortable when I am referred to as British. I have always felt European in my attitudes to life and have always questioned the validity and relevance of the artificial borders that have been created over time, often for reasons of political expediency. I am reluctant to use the term

'Citizen of the World', since this phrase is often thought of as trite and unrealistic nowadays, but I guess it will help to explain where I am coming from. As with many nationalities, xenophobia and racism are never far away, and the British are no exception. As history has shown us in the past, at times of recession, financial and social disturbance creates a situation where many seek to find scapegoats, in order to explain and provide and excuse failures in their own lives. In the past we have seen Jews, gays, travellers and others persecuted, simply because they are perceived to fit the criteria of 'someone to blame'. Post 2008, and the scapegoat has become the European Union and all that it stands for. Concerns about what many see as uncontrolled immigration, widening gaps between the rich and the poor, lack of opportunities for less well-educated groups have all added to this poisonous and destructive debate.

When my partner and I moved to Spain 13 years ago, it was during a period of excitement and positivity towards the new found freedoms that expats such as ourselves were given. We left the UK during a period when anything was possible. The European Union opened the door to new opportunities and a new way of life. Like so many others, we followed well-trodden footprints of many thousands of expats before us who had suddenly realised that the door was now open; we could live and work in any European country that appealed to us. No longer would we need work permits, visas and permissions. Our rights as citizens of Europe would be protected wherever we chose to settle; we could buy property, start businesses and finally take our place as a member within a community of nations. It was when positivity and 'can do' attitudes prevailed, and we were ready to play a full part within it. How quickly things have changed.

During my time working as a newspaper reporter, and later as a columnist and author, I have seen at first hand the benefits that a new life in Spain, France, Portugal, Italy, as well as other countries, have offered British expats, as well as those from many other countries. For some, it has been the promise of starting a new business in a country offering a lifestyle that they can easily empathise with. For others, it has been the promise of a new life in a country offering a freshness and vibrancy to life. For many retired people, a new life in the sun offered the relaxation and health-promoting climate sought for most of their working lives. We have also seen a period of peace, stability and prosperity within Europe that our forefathers would never have thought possible. So, what has gone wrong?

Britain is an island nation and, whether we like it or not, xenophobia has always been part of the British psyche. There has always been an element within British society that has distrusted Europe specifically, and foreigners in general. Some of these attitudes are based upon arrogance, whilst ignorance also plays a large part. Media players, such as the Daily Mail and other popular tabloids have helped to cultivate the 'Hate Europe' theme, fed and nurtured by right wing politicians. The concept of 'Britishness', which stemmed from the Days of the British Empire and nurtured by two World Wars have helped to instil this view subconsciously within the mind-set of many British people. "Let's put the Great back in Britain" was the meaningless cry that was frequently heard during the Brexit debate, in much the same way as "Let's put the Great back in the US" is heard from Trump supporters during the current US Presidential debate.

The global recession also accelerated the view that Britain should leave Europe. Far from being "all in it together", as the previous Prime Minister proclaimed, the post-recession period has led to even greater inequalities in society with the rich becoming richer and the poor getting poorer. In Europe too, social divisions and inequality of the distribution of wealth that we have witnessed in Greece, Spain, Portugal and other countries have led to huge political and financial turmoil, as well as social strife. The European Monetary System and the euro have been blamed for making matters worse, with economists taking the view that the EMS will only work if and when the EU becomes a true political union. This view has sent shockwaves throughout the British Establishment, helping to trigger a view that Britain should leave, unable to face even the vague reality that Europe might become even more politically united.

Unemployment in Europe has led to the jobless in many European countries taking matters into their own hands and moving to countries where greater prosperity is perceived. Anxious to enlarge the European project, former members of Eastern Europe, as well as Greece were allowed to join before they were financially and socially aligned. The wide disparity led to the UK being on the receiving end of too large an influx of workers, which it could not support. Health, education, housing and social services have all come under strain from this rapid influx of migrant workers, which many British people feel is a threat to their own lives and well-being. Sadly, the UK government failed to keep up with rising demand for services and appeared to be ill equipped to support ever-growing communities, whilst at the same time maintaining its determination to promote the mantra of 'austerity' at all costs, when investment in infrastructure and services would have been the more effective option.

The European Union is also to blame and often criticised for being undemocratic and arrogant in its approach. However, a close examination of the structure of the EU by experts reveals that it is far more democratic that current political structures within the UK; one only has to glance at the composition of the House of Lords and the promotion of its sitting members through a discredited honours system to see why. The EU has failed to promote itself, is often seen as too remote and fails to take into account the needs and problems within individual member states. I suspect that if the EU had been more flexible about freedom of movement during times of particular strain, such as in Britain's case, the referendum may never have arisen. The EU was also seen interfering too closely in the day-to-day business of member states. Issues such as the EU's insistence in the straightness of bananas rapidly became the stuff of a tabloid insistence that the EU was out of control; although of course, the banana issue was never true anyway. The media and their readers chose to forget issues such as workers' rights, maternity rights, equality issues and a host of other important measures

# amazon.co.uk

## A gift note from Barrie Mahoney:

*Happy Birthday Kerry! We hope you have a great day and a happy and healthy year ahead. Much love from Barrie, David, Bella and Mac XX*

Gift note included with **Footprints in the Sand (Letters from the Atlantic)**

# amazon.co.uk

SDXdhkDgGk

DXdhkDgGk/-1 of 1-/no-rush-delivery-uk/13978711 A1

Thank you for shopping at Amazon.co.uk!

**Packing slip for**
Your order of 21 November 2016
Order ID 204-9993568-3041938

Packing slip number DXdhkDgGk
Shipping date 21 November 2016

| Qty. | Item | Bin |
|---|---|---|
| 1 | **Footprints in the Sand (Letters from the Atlantic)** Taschenbuch, Mahoney, Barrie 0995602719 ; 0995602719; 9780995602717 | |

This delivery represents part of your gift. The other portion is being sent separately.

31/DXdhkDgGk/-1 of 1-//EFN-EIN8/no-rush-delivery-uk/13978711/1122-10:30/1121-19.44 Pack Type : A1

introduced by the EU. Once again, the EU failed to promote itself and inform the wider public; indeed, general ignorance of the British public about what the EU does was shamefully apparent during the EU referendum debate.

As an educationalist, I know that education too must accept its fair share of blame for Britain's attitudes towards Europe. As a school inspector, very rarely have I seen quality European studies taking place in schools. The quality of teaching in history relating to our joint European heritage has been patchy at best, and ignored at worst. Language teaching in the last twenty or thirty years has become more of an option rather than a necessity in both primary and secondary schools, where the requirement to teach a second language was quietly dropped in recent years; a move mainly designed to reduce costs than to enhance the quality of the curriculum. A focus upon reorganisation and moving the blocks around the table rather than improving what is actually taught to our children has led to whole areas of knowledge being ignored or discarded; the teaching of European languages being one of them. Despite worthwhile projects introduced by the EU, such as the Erasmus Project, most of the nation's young are oblivious to what the EU is about.

In my view, British Governments of all shades have ignored the need to educate the general public about Europe, possibly for their own distorted purpose. In Spain and in many other countries, major projects, such as roads and new buildings are partly or wholly funded by the European Union, and are celebrated as joint European projects, with the flying of the

European flag, references to the EU in literature, and it is clear to everyone who has footed the bill. I have rarely seen any acknowledgement of European Union funding for projects within the UK; I seldom see the flying of the European flag or its logo stating its commitment to a joint European project. No wonder that the general public is mostly ignorant of the part that the European Union plays in everyday life. These are all elements that led to the vote to leave the European Union.

As in previous years, this volume of 'Letters from the Atlantic' covers a twelve-month period of my life as an expat, together with some of the challenges, delights and experiences that many of us face. Brexit has formed part of the concerns and worries during the current year, and so there are some 'Letters' written during this traumatic period. Not all readers will agree with my views relating to Brexit, but such is the nature of strongly held opinions, and particularly when it potentially and significantly affects important parts of lives that we thought were permanently established. Whatever your views, I hope you will enjoy this current volume as expats all over world continue creating 'footprints in the sand'.

# Footprints in the Sand

The Canary Islander

# The Sands of Time

Most of us take sand for granted. Many of us hope that when we go on holiday, we will be able to enjoy a clean beach, with lots of golden sand. If we have deeper pockets, maybe we can head to one of those picture postcard Caribbean resorts offering white sand, or possibly somewhere even closer to home. I know of several beautiful, white sandy beaches in Scotland's Hebridean Islands, although it is usually far too cold to enjoy them to the full. Another option is Spain's Canary Islands, of course, which offer natural white sandy beaches in Fuerteventura, for instance. However, environmentally aware tourists should know than some of the gleaming white sandy beaches in Gran Canaria are not natural, since vast quantities of white sand have been imported from elsewhere, with an accompanying negative cost to the environment.

So what is sand? It is a natural material that has been created from finely ground rock particles. It varies according to its location and its source of rock in the area. Another type of sand has been created over billions of years from various life forms, such as shellfish and coral, as well as from eroded limestone; this is the type of sand that is mostly found in exotic places, such as the Caribbean. The sand on most of the Canary Islands is black, simply because the islands are volcanic in origin. Maybe it is not so nice to look at, but it fulfils broadly the same purpose when building sandcastles.

To the south of Gran Canaria are the Maspalomas Sand Dunes, which are spectacular two square kilometres of sand that originate from coral reefs; the area was declared a Natural Reserve in 1987. Over thousands of years, these have been crushed into fine golden grains of limestone through the grinding action of glaciers. Ocean currents drag the sand to the shore where the wind gathers it into huge and spectacular dunes. The sand is blown inland from the beach, where it accumulates around shrubs. The piles of sand eventually grow larger than the shrubs and gradually move across the field of dunes to create the incredible landscape that we currently enjoy. This is as an ongoing cycle and the reason why the landscape changes, albeit quite slowly, over time and from east to west.

Over the years, the area has become a tourist hotspot, and well known for the beauty of its dunes, as well as for the facilities provided by some of the best hotels in Spain. Sadly, the rapid building development in the area has changed the ongoing cycle of sand. The dunes are now hemmed in by large buildings; instead of the sand moving in a continuous every changing circle, the sand is now blown out to sea. As a result, the quantity of sand is reducing and the dunes are getting smaller. Indeed, it is suggested that within the next century, the dunes could disappear altogether.

Since the dunes are an important tourist attraction and create valuable business for the Canarian economy, plans are currently being discussed by the Island Government to replenish the sand on the dunes by taking it from offshore sandbanks, and before the sand is blown out to the deep water. This will be an expensive and time-consuming process, if it works. The only alternative is removing all the hotels and large buildings in the area, which I guess wouldn't go down too well with hoteliers and tourists alike.

We have yet another example where Island planning has failed to take into account the forces of nature and the need to work with, rather than against, the environment; natural forces always have their way in the end. Maybe a few, smaller hotels built to sensible, low level specifications, as on the Island of Lanzarote, would not have had the grotesque impact that the thousand bed monstrosities have had upon the local environment. Yes, the tourist capacity and income would be much reduced, but at least we would maintain the magnificence of the Maspalomas Sand Dunes.

## Shifting Sand

I'm all for a beautiful white, sandy beach; after all, it is the stuff of postcards, and the kind of image that one dreams about during those cold, wet and rainy days in the UK. I now live in a Gran Canarian village that can only offer black sand on its small, secluded beach. We live on a small volcanic island and the geology of the area dictates the colour of the sand. In contrast, the nearby Maspalomas Dunes, which offers a wonderful, ever changing landscape of shifting near-white sand, is again due to the geological make up of that part of the island. Sadly, not all beaches come supplied with white sand, and that is just the way it is.

We have recently returned from a visit to one of our favourite islands, Fuerteventura. Anyone who has visited this unique island will have noticed the many kilometres of brilliant white sand, set against a stunning blue sea and sky on the outskirts of the bustling tourist resort of Correlejo. This beautiful area is a protected natural park, and is a delight to the eye, as well as being a photographer's paradise. In addition to admiring the white sand, tourists can also enjoy kite and wind surfing and all manner of seaborne activities. If all else fails, nothing beats an afternoon of relaxation well away from the crowds on a near deserted, beautiful beach.

The temptation to provide a white sandy beach to attract tourists is the reason why one of the timeshare companies in Gran Canaria has decided to transform what some may see as a rather dull, pebbly traditional Canarian cove into one of white sand, no doubt to match the blue sea and sky that many holidaymakers dream about. Despite nearly 25 years of protests from locals and environmentalists, permission has finally been granted and the traditional pebbly beach has now been transformed into a gleaming mass of white sand, which has been paid for by the timeshare company.

The only problem with trying to create a white sandy beach close to this timeshare mecca is that there is no gleaming white sand available locally. Therefore, 70,000 tonnes of Saharan sand were purchased and imported from the Western Sahara. Sadly, it now appears that the sand was all but 'stolen' from the displaced people of the Western Sahara; the Sahawari people claim that they were not consulted, and that their natural resources were taken from them without compensation or their permission.

Recently, Saharawi representatives arrived in the Canary Islands to complain that the act of removing the sand was both illegal and criminal, since it belonged to the Saharawi people who were removed from the area by the Moroccan army after Spain abandoned its former colony some 40 years ago.

Environmentalists have consistently warned of the dangers of transporting sand from other regions, since it brings with it the risk of importing non-indigenous species of life into the area, with unknown and unforeseen consequences. We also know from similar experiments on the island that moving sand in this way has caused tortoises, turtles, lizards and many other creatures to be destroyed in the process of sucking up sand for transportation. Has anyone also considered the implications of shifting large quantities of 'alien' sand upon other environmentally sensitive areas along the coastline?

Meanwhile, the timeshare company has plans to develop the site even further by adding a marina and several hotels offering five-star quality with a combined capacity of around 7500 beds. These plans are accompanied by the usual fine words of promise to create more jobs and prosperity for local people, which in reality it rarely does in the long term, since profits are quickly sucked out of the islands and into the coffers of large international conglomerates. It is a project that is unashamedly designed to transform a natural area into a tourist mecca, which indeed it will.

In these times when the price of everything is fully costed, but true value is ignored, there seems to have been little consideration of the environmental costs and impact that such a development will cause. The planners and suits have spoken, so I guess that we will just have to get used to the wilful destruction of yet another part of our beautiful island, even though a white sandy beach does look rather pretty.

I'm just off to the black sand on our small village beach for a swim. It may be black, but at least I know that it is environmentally friendly.

## An Escape to the Island of Los Lobos

It was time again for an escape to one of our neighbouring islands. This time, it was the turn of the small island of Los Lobos (Wolves Island), which is just a short boat trip from Corralejo in the north of Fuerteventura.

There are no wolves on the island, since Los Lobos was named after the large number of monk seals that once lived there in peace. Man, in his usual style, decided to kill them all for food, their fat and skin when the island was discovered in the Fifteenth Century. Monk seals are now all but extinct in the area.

The island became a supply base for the conquest of Fuerteventura in 1405, and until 1968, the only inhabitants of the island were the lighthouse keeper and his family who operated the lighthouse at the northern tip of this small island. I couldn't help but wonder how his children managed to get to school each day, since the sea crossing was a little choppy.

The island is now a natural park, one of the first in the Canary Islands, and is also designated as an area requiring special protection for the many species of marine migratory birds that frequent the island. None of the visitors that I travelled with seemed that interested in migratory birds, but headed off to one of the small beaches for a day of sunbathing and swimming instead.

I was interested in finding out more about a statue of a very forbidding looking woman close to the small quay. The statue was erected in honour of Josefina Pla who was a writer and professor, born on the island in 1909. She later moved to Paraguay in 1927 with her husband, where she developed an extensive and important literary career. Josefina received many awards and distinctions for her literary work for defending human rights and equality for men and women.

Surprisingly, this small island was also of some importance to the Roman Empire. The University of La Laguna in Tenerife, is currently undertaking archaeological investigations on the island to discover more about the activities of the Roman Empire around two thousand years ago. The Roman Empire had control over most of mainland Europe and North Africa, but little has been known about its influence on the Canary Islands until recently.

The island has revealed many Roman artefacts, including hooks and nails made from bronze and iron, plates, cups, lids for cooking pots and handles for kitchen and dinner utensils commonly used by Romans during this period. Archaeologists believe that these findings show that Romans visited this island, as well as other Canary Islands on a seasonal basis, rather than for permanent occupation. So why were they so interested?

Designer fashion in clothing for men and women was as important during Roman times as it is now for the rich and important in society, but purple dye for clothes could only be made from red-mouthed rock shells or sea snails. However, these sea snails are difficult to find, but Roman explorers found them in abundance in the Canary Islands, where they are also known as carnadilla.

Buildings found on Los Lobos appear to have been the processing plants to extract the purple dye from these sea snails that was then used for luxury clothing items that gave a sign of social distinction in Roman Society. These purple dye factories date from the First Century BC to the First Century AD and were found at the south west of the island near to La Concha beach, which is also called La Calera beach.

Archaeological findings such as these are important as they suggest that Roman influence on the Canary Islands could have been more important than previously thought, as historians had believed that the Roman Empire had mostly remained on mainland Spain and North Africa. Coastal regions of Morocco were used by the Romans as a centre for its purple dye industry, which would also link to the Canary Islands in the search for the hard to find, but valuable sea snails.

My brief visit to the island was a wonderful experience and reminded me yet again of the rich variety that we enjoy from all the Canary Islands; each one is unique. Sadly, I didn't get a moment on those much reported beautiful beaches, as I was far too busy taking photographs and exploring the island. Hopefully, I will return again very soon.

# Squirrelogy

My first encounter with a squirrel was not a happy one. I was about five years old, and we had just arrived for my first holiday in Bournemouth, staying with my elderly great aunt in her Victorian home. I still remember entering the old house through a small conservatory that housed many glass cases in which were collections of stuffed birds and animals. I clearly remember several small birds trapped in a frozen, lifeless state behind glass walls; a beautiful fox with its mouth open ready to devour whatever the taxidermist had imagined when preparing the poor creature for display.

The one creature that I still remember in considerable detail was a small red squirrel holding an acorn in its claws staring at me with its lifeless, glass eyes. This squirrel haunted me for my entire holiday and it got to the point where I could not bear to look at the poor creature; I ran whenever I had to pass by to avoid its sad stare. My great aunt's home represented a time when killing and sticking pins into butterflies for display, and installing birds and small animals into glass cases was seen as acceptable. Thankfully, some things have changed for the better.

Several years later, I had the opportunity to become acquainted with red squirrels that have become synonymous with Brownsea Island; that small, enchanted island strategically placed in Poole Harbour, Dorset. Brownsea Island is currently one of the few places in England where red squirrels thrive, although sadly I understand that many are now infected with a form of squirrel leprosy. As a visitor, and later as a teacher escorting hoards of children through the island's woodland, the squirrels' playful charm and shy curiosity always entertained and amused us. They are cautious creatures and only occasionally would they appear, much to the annoyance of my pupils.

When I lived in the UK, I often used to walk through woodlands, as well as more populated areas, such as the seafront gardens in Bournemouth where squirrels of the grey variety, who are even bolder and more curious than their red cousins, would compete with pigeons for pieces of sandwiches, crisps and any other goodies that visitors would offer them. In short, over the years I have fallen for the subtle charms of squirrels, of whatever variety. When we moved to the Canary Islands, I thought I would not see any again. How wrong I was!

During a recent holiday on the Canary Island of Fuerteventura, we came across many squirrels close to Caleta de Fuste, also known as Squirrel Mountain. These squirrels certainly put the UK's grey squirrels to shame in their cheeky boldness as they deftly scamper up the arms of visitors to collect a tasty treat. These squirrels are the Moorish Squirrel or Barbary Ground Squirrel and use their many charms to endear themselves to both the locals and visitors to the island. Due to their trusting and endearing nature, they have become a considerable tourism asset for the island.

Fuerteventura Squirrels, or to be correct Barbary Ground Squirrels, are not native to Fuerteventura, but were accidentally introduced to the island in 1965 as escapee pets. The two pet squirrels quickly bred, the climate and food sources were acceptable and these endearing creatures have now successfully colonised much of the island. Indeed, large yellow and black signs imploring visitors 'Not to feed the squirrels' are now becoming commonplace around the island.

In recent years, there have been serious university studies investigating the environmental impact that these illegal migrants have upon the island; I guess it could be described as a kind of Brexit plot against squirrels. I recall a time when university 'Media Studies' courses were regarded as frivolous and not 'a proper degree', but it seems that any subject can be the focus of degree status nowadays, and a degree in squirrelogy is clearly highly desirable.

In true human compassion, initial conclusions indicated that these delightful creatures should be exterminated and considered as pests. However, at the time of writing, I am pleased to report that after costing this 'remedy', it appears that it would be too expensive, if not impossible to carry out. The focus will now be upon ensuring that these squirrels do not develop a taste for the other Canary Islands and measures are in place to ensure that the more athletic squirrels do not paraglide into the other islands.

For these squirrels, the impact of the global economic crisis has been positive, since it seems to have secured their future in Fuerteventura. Might I also suggest that if this growing population becomes a problem, then some kind of non-harming birth control provided in their nuts might be the way forward?

There is no doubt that, despite squirrelogy, the Fuerteventura squirrel has won its place in the hearts of locals and visitors alike. Officials are only now becoming aware of the publicity value to tourism that these furry migrants bring to the island. Indeed, many are now suggesting that the squirrel becomes the official logo of Fuerteventura.

# Coming or Going?

The Canary Islander

# The European Expat

Cards on the table, I am pro European, and have always been committed to the European project, and would vote to remain in the EU with or without a deal. Frankly, I have found the UK Prime Minister's recent tour of Europe to squeeze a better deal for the UK to be embarrassing, petulant, tinkering, and one that is hard to explain intelligently to European friends and neighbours. The European club is far from perfect, but reform by working together within the club of nations is far more effective than stomping off the pitch and shouting insults at the remaining players.

The EU debate is now one of those areas of life where the passions and debate from both sides of the argument are coming to the fore, and sadly, already creating some unpleasantness. I will not rehearse the already familiar arguments from both sides relating to security, immigration and the economy, since there are many more people who have much greater knowledge and experience of such matters, but will restrict my comments to several issues that would be likely to have an impact upon expats living in Spain.

Currently, expats enjoy the freedom of being able to live and work in any country of their choosing within the EU. Today, I live in the Canary Islands, but tomorrow I could pack my bags and choose to live and work in the Netherlands, Italy, or any of the 28 member states of the EU. Spanish and European law gives foreign residents permanent right to reside once they have been legally resident for five years. Currently, all European expats have this right regardless of the whim of any individual government who, for political reasons, may decide to change the rules. I contrast this to the time before the EU treaty, when work permits had to be applied for and regularly renewed; residency, together with the right to purchase a home in some pre EU countries was severely restricted or near impossible to achieve.

Speaking to older expats who lived through this process, reminds me of visa restrictions that are currently in place for expats living in Thailand and other popular expat destinations; it can be done, but it is not easy. For me, this right of residency has been one of the greatest advantages of being a member of the European Union. Others will say that expats from Switzerland and Norway, who are not within the EU, live quite happily as expats in Spain. This is partly true, but their right to remain in the country is one of individual agreement between governments, subject to political whim and political pressure, and not one of right, which UK expats currently enjoy within the EU.

The reciprocity of health benefits is an area that concerns many expats living in Spain. The current arrangement for health cover being funded by the UK government would cease once the UK left the European Union. Expats would then be responsible for negotiating their own health insurance, or hope that some form of replacement agreement between the Spanish and UK governments would eventually be put into place. Currently, there is a safety net arrangement in place in Spain for those who became legal residents before April 2012, but again, this depends upon the attitude, generosity and financial pressures faced by a future Spanish government; it is not guaranteed. One has only to add the thorny issue of Gibraltar into the equation and the friendly relations that are currently enjoyed by both countries could quickly be soured. I suspect that healthcare would be a major issue of continuing concern for most expats living in Spain.

Many expats rely upon a salary or pension from the UK. As we are already seeing, the value of the pound is falling rapidly and experts warn that this period of instability will continue until the referendum. This uncertainty and instability is already an example of what could happen if the UK left the EU, although eventually the pound could become stronger than the euro once again, but it may remain volatile. Credit rating agencies are already nervous about the UK leaving the EU and forecast a reduction in the UK's credit standing. The credit rating agencies are already warning of both short-term disruptions, as well as long-term implications for the UK's global financial standing.

The UK Government will pay pensions wherever pensioners request, but there are no pension increases for pensioners living outside the EU. UK pensioners would find themselves in a similar position to expats living in Canada or Australia, whereby pensions are frozen at the same rate as when they left the UK. Experts suggest that pensions would be frozen at the rate applicable at the date of the referendum should there be a vote to leave.

Whatever the decision, what is in no doubt is the bumpy ride that we will all have to endure until June

23rd. As with all organisations, the European Union needs to recognise its imperfections and adapt to current conditions and the demands of citizens. Hopefully, this can be achieved though listening, discussion and mature negotiation. From the expat point of view, given the many financial, political and humanitarian issues that the World is currently facing, now is not the time to take a leap off the cliff.

## Brexit - 'The Facts'

The current debate about whether or not the UK should leave the European Union has already led to some ill tempered, and often poorly informed debates. The comment that continues to both amuse and irritate me is the now common cry heard on TV and radio programmes "We don't know how to vote; we need more facts." Well the sad truth is, and it will be cold comfort for some, but there aren't any real 'facts' to share.

Since the debate about 'Brexit' began, I have received many questions from expats who are genuinely troubled about their future lives in Europe. Many questions relate to their right of residency and employment, health care, passports, pensions, driving licences, as well as property ownership. Sadly, I do not know the answers and, frankly, no one does. I may have an opinion that I will share with readers from time to time, and when any concrete information comes my way, I will pass it on.

In the end, I suspect that all we can do is listen to people, such as politicians that we trust and respect (if there are any), listen to both sides of the debate, and try to be as well informed as we can about what the European Union is truly about, and vote as our hearts and minds tell us. Either way, the genie is out of the bottle, and whatever the result, I doubt that things will ever be quite the same again for expats living in Europe. Certainly, it has little do with 'facts' that are as illusive as snowdrops in summer.

Everything evolves over time, and the EU is no exception. Whatever the decision, we may or may not be heading towards a brighter future. What we can be certain of is that our relationship with the European Union will change, and be different from what we currently know. The truth is that we know what we have, or think we have, with the European Union as it is currently formed. What we don't know, and no one does, is what the UK's departure from this club of European nations will actually look like in the case of a potential Brexit.

What we are hearing during the debates and endless column inches written in newspapers are, of course, merely opinions; opinions, which some may call scaremongering, whilst others will present them as 'facts', which is plainly a nonsense. We do not know, for instance, how the remaining 27 members of the European Union will treat expats living in their countries. I suspect that, in the case of Brexit, the UK will eventually negotiate individual health, pensions and social care deals with other member states, and surely Spain, France, Portugal and Italy will be the main priority, since this is where most expats reside? However, this is merely my opinion, and not a 'fact', and should be treated as such.

Deals affecting the residential and employment status of thousands of expats will take time, and will no doubt not be a high priority, given the many other urgent pressures facing the UK Government that would inevitably follow Brexit, but some kind of deal will happen - eventually. Once again, this is merely an opinion, and not a fact. Will we need work permits to work in Spain? Will UK pensions continue to be index linked? They may, or may not - no one knows for sure. Meanwhile, I suspect that expats will be in for an uncertain, if not rough ride for a few years. I am already hearing stories from businesses, ranging from estate agents, furniture outlets, removals and travel companies in Spain reporting that business from would be and current expats has reduced sharply. If nothing else, the current debate has shaken confidence that will put off the decision for many would be expats to move to a new life in the sun until the referendum is over.

So if anyone tells you that their information is 'a fact', or you hear such claims on TV or read it in the newspaper, please read it with extreme caution, and don't believe a word of it. This current demand for 'facts' reminds me of a comment that my father would often mutter when he was told that something was a fact. "A fact is a lie and a half" was always his response. Now I know what he meant; I suspect that he was right.

# Referendum? What Referendum?

This is an anxious time for many expats. The question of whether or not the UK will remain as a member of the European Union is an issue that many thought would never arise.

The number of expats living overseas seems to be shrouded in mystery and depends much upon which side of the argument is reporting these so called 'facts'. It is widely thought that there are about 750,000 expats living in Spain, which vastly outweighs those living in any other European country. The issues about what will happen whether or not the UK remains in Europe matters to a significant number of people who have made their lives in a country of their choice, and not merely where they happen to have been born.

Amidst all the scare stories from both sides of the argument, there are very few real facts to hand. Indeed, I would be hard pressed to name even one fact with absolute certainty. Meanwhile, we are assured by what used to be a reliable media heavyweight, the Times, that British expats are packing their bags and heading back to the White Cliffs of Dover in droves. Figures of around 100 expats a day are being quoted. However, what these 'statistics' fail to report is that there are many more would be expats leaving the UK each day and heading to a new life in the sun. Of course, it is not in anyone's interest to report this, is it?

How do we know this? Important data relating to Spain's economy, which is usually conveniently ignored by the UK, reveals that the country's economy is recovering well, with a gross domestic product forecast outperforming both the UK and Germany. The International Monetary Fund has hailed Spain for its remarkable economic rebound, and overseas property buyers, particularly from the UK, are returning in large numbers. House prices and availability of rental properties are usually reliable indicators, and estate agents in the Costas are currently reporting that property sales and rentals are once again doing very well. Although this activity is not at the pre-2008 crazy levels, house prices are increasing at a sensible rate, and particularly in the favoured areas of Valencia, Catalonia, the Balearics and the Canary Islands. The Brits are once again in the lead in both purchasing and renting properties in these most popular areas. Enquiries and hits on expat websites, as well as enquiries to removals companies, are also demonstrating a rapid increase in activity from would-be expats intent upon heading across the Channel.

What about established expats? The idea that established expats are being frightened back to the UK, 'just in case', is nonsense. There has always been a flow of those heading to Europe and those returning to the UK, because of ill health, relationship breakdowns, business failure or homesickness, which will always continue. I know of many established expats who are considering a number of options, should the worst happen, including opting for Spanish citizenship, or relying upon a passport from another European country. One example of this is the large number of UK expats who already have, or are applying for an Irish passport.

Currently, even the vague threat of British exit from the European Union has not put off would be expats to head to a new life in the sun. Referendum? What referendum? It'll take much more than a bureaucratic and divisive exercise, masquerading as democracy, to stop a Brit from living his or her dream in the sun.

## Slipping into an Alternative Universe

As a long-term fan of the BBC TV series, Doctor Who (the Russell T Davies period, to be precise), I have thought a lot about the good Doctor this week. It has been an interesting week for British expats, raising many important issues and possible consequences, as well as opportunities, depending upon which side of the debate you are coming from. Returning to Doctor Who, I cannot help but recall the series when The Master took over as Prime Minister of Britain, which shortly afterwards became a severe threat to the entire World. The sad thing was that the general population, the British voter, did not know why they were voting for him. They had entered into some kind of trance-like state, and were being controlled and manipulated by a malevolent force that they did not understand. Fortunately, the good Doctor came to the rescue just in time...

This week, I have felt that I have slipped into an alternative universe, and not a pleasant one either. Although the EU Referendum vote did not go as I personally would have wished, like many it has left me surprised, confused, saddened and ashamed. Although I understand why many Brits voted as they did, as there is no doubt that the free movement of people in Europe continues to be a major issue in the UK, I fail to see how an exit from the EU will significantly address the problem. Leading Brexit politicians now also seem to be backtracking on this issue too; I had assumed that they would have a plan. We continually hear cynical references to "the will of the people", but most of us already know that it is the will of the media, rich and powerful that really matters.

I have been a strong supporter of the European project for all of my adult life, and will continue to do so. My partner and I chose Spain as our country of choice many years ago, mainly for health reasons, and we have not been disappointed. Mostly, the experience has been rewarding and enriching, but it has been challenging too. Together, we have faced a number of issues, but overall, Spain and the Canary Islands have been very good to us. We quickly found work, a home and new friends from a variety of European nations. When we lost our jobs, the Spanish Government paid us generous unemployment benefit, a percentage of our salaries that was limited to the amount that we had paid into the system. It gave us time to reduce our outgoings and adjust to finding new work. During our time of unemployment, we were offered language courses that were free of charge, with offers of additional courses and training if required; the social security system could not have been more supportive. When my partner became ill, the Spanish Health Service offered superb support from the doctor in our village, the local emergency health centre, as well as the hospital. When I needed a series of eye operations that even London´s Moorfields Eye Hospital could not provide, I received excellent specialist care in the Canary Islands that took care of complicated issues that has saved my sight. For all this, I will always be grateful.

Like most people, I dislike rapid change, because experience tells me that 'change in haste' leads to 'repenting at leisure'. I applaud those expats who have sought to protect their legal status in the country by applying for Spanish citizenship, or taking full advantage of the right to apply for an Irish, Maltese or Romanian passport. Personally, I will be doing nothing at all, but waiting and watching developments. There is no rush, and Brexit will not happen for another two years, if it ever happens at all. I was born British and fully intend to die British, and not an amalgam of passport anomalies and conveniences. Mind you, I will never say never, because I have learned that fate often has a nasty way of making me eat my words.

That old saying on our fridge magnet comes to mind, 'Keep Calm and Carry On'. As I pour myself another glass of wine and head out for another dose of Canarian sunshine, I really cannot help but wonder if and when the good Doctor will come to save us from the evil plans of The Master...

## Life Between the Devil and the Deep Blue Sea

Despite the doom and gloom forecast by many following the UK's surprise Brexit vote, it appears that it will take more than Brexit to dissuade many thousands of Brits intent upon heading to a new life in the sun.

Latest quarterly reports show that property prices in Spain are at least stabilising, and in many cases bouncing back, to the levels last seen in 2007 and 2008. This trend varies from region to region with increases seen in 30 of Spain's 50 provinces. The most significant property price increases have recently been seen in La Rioja (7.4%), Catalunya (6.8%), Madrid (5.4%) and the Canary Islands (3.6%).

My own limited discussions with estate agents in the Canary Islands, the Costa Blanca and the Costa del Sol also report a positive rather than negative outlook regarding property prices and the continued, if not increasing, interest from Brits anxious to begin a new life in Spain.

Many had assumed that following the Brexit vote, interest from potential expats would decrease until the position with the European Union stabilised. However, judging from the rapid increase in traffic to 'The Canary Islander' website and, in particular the 'Living and Working in Spain and the Canary Islands' pages, it is clear that the reverse has happened, where web traffic has trebled in the two weeks following the vote. Emails and correspondence from would-be expats indicate that many have decided to 'leap' across the Channel before the gates close, if that happens, as well as activity fuelled by disillusionment from what many see as the UK rapidly turning into an insular parody of 'Little Britain'.

It is good to see so many expats making decisions to secure their future within Europe, with the Irish Embassy having to take on more staff in the rush created by British expats attempting to obtain Irish passports, as well as considerable interest in applying for Spanish, French or Italian citizenship, for those who meet the relevant criteria.

During the run up to the EU Referendum, it is true that many people, and particularly the elderly, sick and those who live alone, reviewed their futures as expats living within a Europe that would not include the UK. These concerns continue, and a number have written to tell of their concerns about disturbing a life that they had always considered as settled for the remainder of their lifetimes. Many simply do not have sufficiently good health or financial resources to return to the UK, and their entitlement to services in the UK lapsed long ago. In some ways, these elderly expats are literally trapped between the devil and the deep blue sea, and early clarification from the UK Government is anxiously awaited.

Far from confidence in an expat life reducing, early evidence suggests that confidence and determination in working towards an expat life is increasing. Although it is still too early to be clear about the motivation of many and to predict where this trend will lead, I suspect that disillusionment with the instability of the UK's political process, as well as widespread disagreement about the UK's future within Europe is leading many to vote with their feet. It will be interesting to see how this develops in the months and years ahead.

## Brexit is Good for Europe

As distasteful as the EU referendum has been for many, the referendum process may have been a positive event in ways that were not at first expected. During the 40 plus years that the UK has been a member of the EU, many Europeans have taken its many benefits for granted. In the last decade, there has been considerable and growing apathy towards an expanding European project, which UKIP, the media and cynics have exploited to their full advantage.

Before the referendum, I rarely heard the EU being discussed in a positive light, and those of us who strongly believe in the European project, albeit reformed, have tended to keep their views to themselves. How events over the last few weeks have changed the topic of conversation and all manner of discussion in our national life. For the first time that I can remember, I am regularly hearing positive comments, as well as negative, being articulated wherever I go; this is a healthy development.

Britain's reluctance to be a full and enthusiastic member of the EU has always been a controversial issue and I suspect that in time, historians will reflect upon the strong opposition of France's President de Gaul, who was strongly opposed to the UK's membership of the Common Market in the 1960s. Maybe he was right in his judgement that Britain was not and never will be European in attitude, and that the insular views of an island community will always prevail.

When I moved to Spain, and later to the Canary Islands, I was surprised to see public recognition of the EU's influence upon the country happily and generously acknowledged. Many forget that it was the EU that supported Spain's painful transition from Franco's cruel dictatorship to that of a modern democracy that we see today. Major infrastructure projects, such as new roads, bridges and tunnels are always readily acknowledged, including the flying of three flags: the Spanish flag, the Canarian flag and the European flag. No one is ever in any doubt that these projects have been funded partially or fully by the European Union. Frankly, I have rarely seen similar acknowledgement in the UK of the many projects funded by the EU. As a result, the general public are oblivious and mostly left ignorant of exactly what the EU contributes to their society. Education too must take its fair share of the blame for the public's antipathy towards the EU.

During the EU referendum, it was the often stated and cynical wish of many Brexit politicians that the UK's 'wisdom' in voting for Brexit would cause remaining EU nations to consider their futures within the EU. Much was and continues to be said about the EU rapidly imploding on the basis that the project is doomed following the UK's decision to leave. However, from my understanding of the European press, and those that I speak to, I suspect that the opposite is happening. For the first time in many years, I hear people talking about the EU positively, and appalled at the UK's decision to go it alone. For the first time I hear people talking and writing about the achievements of the EU, ranging from the peace that it has inspired since the Second World War, and its support and nurturing of democracy in countries entering from the failed Soviet Union. The European Union is by no means perfect, but for the first time many European commentators are talking of a climate of change within the EU, which Brexit has inadvertently encouraged, for the better.

Many European commentators are now seeing Brexit as an opportunity to re-evaluate the values and purposes of this community of nations. Although the UK has contributed much to the debate over the years, it is clear that its continual negativity, stances on renegotiation, cynicism and refusal to accept shared community values has had a negative impact upon the EU's development and reform. Without the UK, many see the EU as finally being in a position to fulfil its potential.

Unlike what is published in the UK media, the European project is not dead, and many European commentators think that Brexit has been a good thing in revealing to Europeans what they may lose should they also choose to follow the Brexit route. I never thought that I would congratulate the result of a Brexit vote, but in the wider context, I suspect that the vote to leave may have done all true Europeans a great favour.

## Ever Been Bumped?

No, I don't mean a minor car accident or one of those over enthusiastic birthday playground 'celebrations' when you were at primary school, but being denied access to a flight when you have already purchased your ticket and all set to fly off on holiday. This has happened to me on a couple of occasions, which left a lot of unanswered questions. After all, how can a flight be 'over booked' when I have bought a ticket?

The first time that this happened to me was a flight from the UK to Barcelona. We had arrived at the airport later than usual; when I say 'later than usual' I mean less than the usual two hours before flying. After all, I do like to check out the condition of the plane before I step aboard... No, we were still in good time and in a very long queue waiting for the usual fun and games at the check-in desk. This is the part that I usually hate, because I invariably have to pay a fee for excess baggage before I set off.

Suddenly, an agitated young woman, wearing a very smart uniform appeared and waved a handful of twenty pound notes in front of me. She explained that if I would care to delay my flight for a couple of hours I would be generously compensated for my trouble. That compensation turned out to be two hundred pounds, a complementary sandwich and a couple of drinks in the bar. Initially, I was hesitant, but the young woman explained that the flight was overbooked and that one of the passengers had to return to Barcelona urgently due to a family bereavement. I would also be given a business upgrade on the next flight, two hours later. The details of the arrangement seemed a little vague, but I felt sorry for my fellow passenger. In the light of the serious issue, a delay of a couple of hours, complete with more than adequate compensation seemed a fair deal, to which I agreed. However, I didn't understand why the flight was overbooked.

A few months later, the same thing happened again, but this time to another destination and from another airport. Strangely enough, I received a similar explanation about the flight being overbooked, a family bereavement and the need for a fellow passenger to take my seat for which I would be amply compensated. On this occasion, I would receive a cash 'thank you', as well as overnight hotel accommodation and breakfast at the airline's expense, since there were no flights until the following day.

On this occasion, I refused the offer; for several reasons. As a teacher, I had been through a difficult school term; I was exhausted and couldn't wait to fly out of the UK as quickly as possible. I was not about to lose one day of my precious holiday. I also felt irritated by the fact that the flight was overbooked, yet again. How was this possible? Surely, tickets were bought and paid for based upon the number of seats? I could not understand how a basic supply and demand situation could fall apart in this way. Although I felt sympathy for the circumstances of my fellow passenger, this time I didn't really believe the story that I was told. Anyway, I had a sun bed and a large gin and tonic waiting for me...

It was many months later that I was chatting to a pilot who was resting before his return flight, that I raised the question of being 'bumped'. This, I gather, is the term for circumstances when passengers agree, or are coerced, into changing their flight. In some cases, there is no negotiation and passengers are merely told that they cannot fly. The pilot's comments were quite illuminating.

Apparently, most airlines deliberately overbook their flights, which is usually by around ten per cent, sometimes more. The main reason is that some passengers simply do not turn up. To my mind, why should that matter? After all, the airline has already sold the ticket so whether the passenger turns up or not is immaterial. My pilot friend pointed out that, in most cases, the airlines will have to offer a free flight or a refund to their would-be passenger if, for instance, they were stuck in traffic or arrived shortly after the gates had closed. In these circumstances, the airlines would lose money and so they put a lot of effort into trying to guess exactly how many people will turn up for their flight. Airlines also like to put aside tickets for last minute business travellers in order to charge higher prices for the privilege.

It is at this point where the problems begin, if the airline has misjudged the popularity of a particular flight. In these circumstances, airlines attempt to persuade passengers to take another flight in return for a voucher, cash, free meals or hotel accommodation, which happened in my case. If everyone has checked in and you have a seat that is confirmed, then there is nothing to be concerned about. However, if the flight is overbooked and there are no volunteers, passengers may be forcibly 'bumped' from a flight, whether they like it or not. I understand that, in these circumstances, compensation is even more generous.

My pilot friend also advised me that the longer the delay, the greater the benefits for volunteers. Compensation usually starts low and continues to rise until someone offers to get 'bumped'. So, the message is that if you really do feel the urge to give up your seat to someone in need, you could earn quite a lot of cash, vouchers, a free meal or hotel accommodation. Indeed, it might even pay for your next flight to the sun.

# Food and Drink

## The Long, Lazy Lunch

Once upon a time there was a Spanish civil servant, an engineer, who was asked to collect an award after 20 years of loyal service to the Spanish state. On further investigation by his superiors, it turned out that he had not appeared for work for the last six years, although this could possibly be as many as fourteen years, no one is quite sure. Someone seemed to remember him popping out for lunch one day, but then all recollections of him after his siesta appear rather hazy.

The 69-year-old engineer 'worked' for a Spanish municipality, but was later seconded to the local water board where he was asked to supervise a waste water treatment plant - quite an important job given that the good people of the municipality rather appreciate having clean water. Fast forward to 2012 when the engineer was due to collect a long service award. This was when the deputy mayor, who had recruited him in 1990, wondered where he was. He hadn't seen the engineer for some time, yet he was on the payroll. Maybe he had died?

No, the engineer had not died, but was living quite happily and continuing to draw his annual salary of around 27,000 euros. The engineer was eventually found and challenged, but could not answer a few basic questions, such as "What did you do yesterday?" or even "What did you do last month?" The engineer, who was suffering from depression, was stuck for words.

This week, a court fined the engineer the equivalent of one year of his annual salary, since it seems that he had not occupied his office for at least six years, although it could be as many as fourteen years. No one had noticed or, it seemed, cared.

In his defence, the engineer claimed that he might not have kept business hours, since he was the victim of workplace bullying; he had a family to support and felt that he would not get another job. In their defence, the council thought the engineer was the responsibility of the water board, whilst the water board thought that he was the responsibility of the municipality. It was rather a grey area.

Meanwhile, I am wondering who was the engineer's line manager, and whether they skipped work as well? Of greater concern to the good people of the municipality, I imagine, is whatever happened to supervising the waste water treatment plant? Maybe the water quality in that area has been a little suspect for the last fourteen years?

Anyway, readers will be pleased to know that the engineer put his spare time to very good use. He spent it by studying philosophy and is now an expert on the works of Spinoza, the Dutch philosopher to whom we give thanks for laying the foundations of the Enlightenment. That's all right then. I always did like a happy ending, although I really cannot say whether the engineer received the long service award, and yes, this is a true story.

## Black Tomatoes, Golden Kiwi and Red Bananas

We grow excellent tomatoes in the Canary Islands, but have you noticed the wide range of colours that are now available? Yellow, orange, red and black tomatoes in abundance appear on most supermarket shelves. I still cannot bring myself to buy black tomatoes; the colour seems completely wrong for a tomato and I really cannot see them successfully adorning a salad. Still, there are always so many on supermarket display shelves, and I assume that some people want to buy them.

I had an unfortunate incident in a local supermarket last week concerning a pack of kiwi fruit. I was in a hurry, and without checking the fruit carefully, placed a pack of fruit in my basket. When I reached the cashier, I noticed that the fruit were a strange yellow colour, instead of the dirty brownish-green shade that I am used to. I raised this with the cashier, pointing out that they were "off" and could I replace them with a pack of fruit that was fit for sale. The cashier looked bemused, but the lady waiting behind me kindly intervened and pointed out that the fruit that I thought had "gone off" was in fact a very desirable new variety of golden fruit from New Zealand. She urged me to try them and assured me that they were much tastier that the usual variety, and that I would come to prefer them. She was right, despite them being the wrong colour.

I have also been hearing quite a lot about red bananas recently. Apparently, the good banana growers of

Tenerife are getting very excited about the possibility of red banana production on the island. I know of one grower who already has a large number of plants in cultivation, and is looking forward to improving the profitability of his plantation in the near future.

Being somewhat of a traditionalist, I like my bananas to be yellow, tomatoes to be red, and my kiwi to be dirty greenish-brown. Even so, being the latest fad, I thought that I had better find out a little more about the subject as I suspect that this new variety will soon be sweeping across the Canary Islands shortly, and at a premium price.

I should confess here that I have never tasted a red banana, but I gather that they are very popular in Central America and the US. Indeed, they became popular in Canada in the 1870s, and appeared some time before the yellow variety in Toronto. I am told that they look amazing in a banana split, can be eaten roasted or fried and are very prolific in their growth, which is good news for growers looking to maximise profits. Apparently, they can be eaten as a tasty savoury, as in Cuba where they are sold as banana chips and eaten rather as you would a bag of chips from the local chippy.

Red bananas, or more correctly named, the Red Dacca, have a reddish purple skin with a flesh that is light pink in colour when ripe. They are sweeter and softer than yellow bananas with just a hint of mango in flavour. For the health conscious, red bananas contain more Vitamin C and beta-carotene than the yellow banana.

Red bananas are eaten in the same way as yellow bananas, and usually eaten raw, chopped or whole. They can be added to fruit salads, desserts, as well as toasted or fried. Red bananas may also be found as a dried product in some speciality shops.

In many ways, I would hate to see the traditional Canarian banana swept aside by this brash newcomer. With its intense, sweet creamy flavour, the traditional Canarian variety is already unique in the world of mass banana production and marketing. The Canarian banana is now marketed as a premium fruit, due to its smaller carbon footprint, juicy flavour and high moisture levels. Maybe the time has come to be a little more adventurous and succumb to the delights of the black tomato, golden kiwi and red banana?

## Fuyu for You

I am sure that we have heard and read more than enough about Brexit, so let's get back to what is really important in life – fruit and vegetables.

One of the delights of living in the Canary Islands and Spain is that we often come across different fruit and vegetables from those normally seen in most British supermarkets. Unless you happen to pop into that wonderful emporium of fruit and vegetables, Harrods, with plenty of spare cash, there are some varieties of amazing fruit and vegetables that are not usually seen in most British supermarkets.

I discovered the "Fruit of the Gods" the other day. More accurately known as persimmon or Sharon Fruit, this delectable fruit has been tempting me for a while, but somehow I didn't have the courage to try one. As feeble as this may sound, I have been caught by strange fruit and vegetables before, and the prickly pear being a particular unfortunate experience, which is a story for another time. One thing that I have learned from that particular experience is always to check with someone knowledgeable about how to prepare, cook and eat any strange new fruit and vegetables that we may come across, and to be clear about what is to be done with anything prickly.

The persimmons that were on display were a joy to look at, and were just asking for a photo shoot. They looked rather like huge, highly polished, orange tomatoes with an overgrown stalk. I was also taken aback by the price, which brought the fruit into the apple and pear price bracket. Remembering the prickly pear experience, I decided to investigate further and asked one of the sales assistants how I should prepare and eat it. The sales assistant nodded and grabbed one of the largest and most luscious fruit on display, beckoned me over to the sink where she carefully washed the fruit. She then took a knife and cut the fruit into slices, passing one to me, as well as to two other passing customers. She took the last piece for herself and started to eat it. Her facial expression was enough to convince me that this was truly the "Fruit of the Gods" as I tucked into the large piece that she had passed to me.

We all commented upon the deliciousness and sweetness of the fruit, which I thought was a cross between a pear in texture and a peach in flavour. However, please don't take my word for it, as other people have given me very different descriptions of the taste; I guess it just depends upon your personal taste buds. I was smitten by this new fruit and bought several to take home.

To complicate matters further, there are several different varieties for sale, but the one usually grown in Spain and the Canary Islands is the tomato-shaped fuyu, or Sharon fruit, with its distinctive orange skin. You can eat a firm fuyu rather like an apple, or wait a week or two until it turns a deep orangey red when you can tuck into its luscious, creamy flesh with a spoon. There is another variety, the hachiya, which has a pointed shape; I am told to avoid eating this like an apple, since its flesh can make your mouth horribly dry due to the tannins in its flesh, and you will spend the next few hours with a mouth feeling like a cheese grater.

The persimmon is the national fruit of Japan, although it has been tampered with in recent years to produce varieties that offer vanilla, chocolate, cinnamon and even pumpkin flavours. For the health conscious, persimmons are fat-free and a good source of vitamins A and C, as well as being a good source of fibre. Personally, I think they are a great find and richly deserve to be called the "Fruit of the Gods".

## The All-Inclusive Wristband

Recent news articles about asylum seekers in Cardiff being forced to wear brightly coloured wristbands in order to claim their meals each day rightly drew both amazement and disgust from many decent people in the UK. This news broke within a few days of the 'Middlesbrough red door' controversy, whereby the homes of asylum seekers were targeted because all their front doors were painted red. Again, many people complained that this policy was wrong. Both incidents revealed an appalling lack of sensitivity towards people who require help and support during a desperate time in their lives.

The issue surrounding brightly coloured wristbands in the Welsh capital drew particular disgust, since any refusal to wear the wristband would simply mean no food. Some likened it to the enforced Star of David symbol, which was used by Nazi Germany to easily identify the Jews. The forced identification of any part of human society in this manner is both degrading and inhuman, and I can understand the disgust and public outcry that both incidents caused.

On a lighter note, I have never understood why so many visitors staying in hotel complexes in the Canary Islands, as well as other tourist complexes in other parts of Spain, are content to wear wristbands, similar to those offered to the Cardiff asylum seekers, which identifies them as 'Breakfast', 'Breakfast and Dinner' or the 'gold standard' of 'All-Inclusive'. Now, I know that Madge and her family in the television comedy 'Benidorm' are quite happy to feast upon all that is offered for 24 hours a day, but do real holidaymakers actually want everyone else to know about it? In any case, do they really want to go home with a white 'lack of sun' ring on their wrists to tell everyone that were 'all-inclusive' characters performing in 'Benidorm'?

I am not a great lover of the 'all-inclusive' deal. Yes, I know it is a godsend for those on a very tight budget, and particularly when travelling with children. I also know of the damage that it causes to restaurants, bars and other small businesses trying to survive on the islands when faced with competition from the 'all-inclusive' hotels, which are financed and backed by large companies with profits funnelled well away from these islands.

I too have been tempted by 'all-inclusive' deals on a couple of occasions, and had a very good time knowing that I could eat and drink without spending another euro for the duration of my holiday, but in the long term, is it really worth it? In addition, the boredom of eating in the same place, at the same table, with more of less the same buffet offerings each day made me feel as if I was in prison rather than on holiday. As for the obligatory wristband, I refused to wear it and, as with the asylum seekers, was briskly informed that I either wore it or didn't eat. I decided to wear it, but later cut it off, and devised a system with the help a piece of gum that would allow me to wear it only at meal times and remove it afterwards; unlike the asylum seekers, I got away with it.

Allegedly, the asylum seekers were threatened with being reported to the Home Office if they did not wear their wristbands and their claims for asylum would be rejected. Others suffered verbal and physical abuse from motorists and passers-by who spotted the wristbands. Life for the asylum seeker is hard enough without some heartless 'jobsworth' threatening to take away their only means of survival. Thankfully, on this occasion, common sense seems to have prevailed and both red painted doors and wristbands are to be dispensed with.

Now back to the 'all-inclusive' deals; may I politely suggest that hotels do away with wristbands and maybe consider some other form of ready identification that is less crude? How about retinal identification or thumbprints, or a quick flash of an app on the mobile phone that goes everywhere?

# Getting to Know You

The Canary Islander

**El Gordo - The Spanish Christmas Lottery**

I had almost forgotten that it was 22 December as I walked down the main shopping street of our nearest town. It was when I heard the endless chanting of numbers sung by children that I remembered it was El Gordo Day! This is the day when 'The Fat One' may deliver a surprise that will change the lives of those who have bought a ticket for the largest lottery in Spain, and the richest in the World.

El Gordo is the second oldest lottery in the World, with the first lottery taking place on 22 December 1812 in Cadiz; it has taken place on the same day ever since. Spaniards may queue for hours to get the chance to buy tickets for this famous Christmas lottery. I was recently very puzzled when I saw a queue stretching throughout the length of a commercial centre. I wondered what the fuss was about until I realised that the queue ended at the lottery kiosk with one harassed sales assistant trying to deal with hundreds of purchasers.

In many ways, El Gordo is the start of Christmas for many Canarians and Spaniards. Initially, I was surprised to see how quiet the street was, but when I peered in many cafe bars and shops, I could see dozens of punters crowded around TV screens, radios and laptops. I have never bought a ticket for a variety of reasons, and find it difficult to understand the fascination of El Gordo. It has also taken me some time to understand the process of buying a ticket.

One ticket costs 200 euros, although most people buy one tenth of a ticket for 20 euros if purchased from authorised outlets, or 22 euros if bought elsewhere. To make it even more confusing, numbers are also divided into series, there are 1600 tickets with the same number sold at lottery sales points across the country, making it impossible for one person to buy them all. Many people buy smaller stakes to increase their chances of winning. A one-euro stake in the winning number is worth 20,000 euros, whilst a 20-euro ticket will pay out 400,000 euros before taxes are deducted.

Now for a few facts and figures. This year, the prize money was 2.2 billion euros, and the odds of winning are put at around one in six, which is possibly why this lottery has the nation gripped on the morning of the 22 December each year. Around 75 per cent of the population enjoys a Christmas flutter, spending 0.3 per cent of Spain's gross domestic product (3.2 billion euros). It is estimated that each Spaniard will spend around 63 euros on tickets for the lottery.

Back to the children singing their tuneless dirge on the nation's TV screens. Every 22 December, the streets of Spain become silent as most people are occupied in watching the draw, which can take up to three hours. The lottery balls are drawn, and the numbers sung by the pupils of Madrid's San Ildefonso School, which was originally a school for orphans, with El Gordo donating a portion of the profits to the school. Originally, the balls were only drawn and sung by boys, but in these more enlightened times, girls now play an equal part in the activity. The audience, both at the live event and at home, often dress up in lottery themed hats and clothes. On a more sour note, in these recessionary times, the Spanish Government now taxes the lottery with a 20 per cent tax on all winnings over 2,500 euros.

Taxman aside, this story ends on a happy note. Ngame and his wife fled Senegal eight years ago on a rickety boat carrying 65 migrants. They were rescued by the Spanish coastguard and arrived in the Canary Islands before later moving to Almeria to find work. The couple found temporary low paid work as vegetable pickers before losing their jobs a few days ago. They have just received the wonderful news that they have won the top prize of 400,000 euros in this year's lottery.

It may be best to avoid Christmas shopping on the morning of the 22 December in future. No one really wants to serve you; they are far too busy dreaming of their big win!

## Making a Difference

I was talking with my ophthalmic consultant the other day. He had just returned from what I thought was a two-week holiday in Bolivia. During our discussion it appears that he was not enjoying a two-week vacation, but was actually working voluntarily in Bolivia for a charity dedicated to improving the eyesight of Bolivian people who do not have ready access to the benefits that we take for granted in Europe. My ophthalmic consultant had spent his holiday treating cataracts and the eye disease, glaucoma. Indeed, he and his companions had travelled to the country with six suitcases of spectacles, something that we often take for granted, but not easily and cheaply available to the indigenous people in that country.

The Canary Islands and mainland Spain have an excellent medical health service, and doctors and nurses are highly trained, experienced and use modern technology for all health issues faced by patients in these regions. However, not all countries in the world can offer all their citizens effective medical treatment, and one of these countries is Bolivia in South America. Doctors in the Canary Islands recognised that indigenous communities in countries, such as Bolivia, face social, geographical and economic problems in gaining access to basic medical care.

A group of medical professionals from the Canary Islands made their first visit to the Amazonian region of Bolivia in 2002 to see how they could offer some practical medical solutions to problems faced by people in remote locations on an effective basis that would be continuous. The result was to establish Solidaridad Medica Canaria in 2003, which would focus on giving health care to people that seemed to be forgotten in the world by working with volunteer medical staff from the Canary Islands who gave up their holidays to work with volunteers in Bolivia.

Later, other regions of Spain joined this medical charity initiative, and in 2006 the name changed to Solidaridad Medica. This charity provides a regular health care programme that serves 74 communities in Bolivia across three regions of the Amazon that are served locally by Solidaridad Medica Bolivia that works with local medical professionals and volunteers.

This charity is funded by private donations and grants from various administrations in Spain and France, but is not a government department or receives Canarian or Spanish government funding. The regions of Spain that provide grants are the Canary Islands, Murcia, Oviedo, Palma, Malaga, Barcelona and Madrid, but the charity also has to rely on private donations from the general public.

One important difference with the charity Solidaridad Medica, when matched against the activities of other well known medical aid charities, is that all funds received from private donations and from regions of Spain are spent on health care for the indigenous people in the Amazon regions of Bolivia, and not on administration.

This charity started in the Canary Islands and has since been very successful in helping others in need, which is a wonderful testament to the dedicated team of medical professionals that help us in the Canary Islands and Spain. If you would like further information about Solidaridad Medica, or are interested in making a donation to help their valuable work, please go to: http://www.solidaridadmedica.org

# The Domino Effect

Have you played dominoes recently? I certainly haven't and, thinking about it, the last time that I played must have been when I was aged nine or ten, recovering from chickenpox and playing the game with my mother during the boring days when I was confined to bed.

During the years that we have lived in the Canary Islands and the Costa Blanca, I often see groups of elderly men sitting together on the pavement, outside a cafe bar, playing dominoes. In most cases, this is not a genteel game played in silence, but quite an energetic activity that involves a lot of shouting and waving of arms. There is one particular group of players that I often see when I pass a cafe bar in our nearest town; it is usually the same group of elderly, and not so elderly men. The game seems to go on for hours.

Yesterday, I noticed that two other tables had joined the usual single table and there was an intense level of interest. I am not sure whether the group were holding some form of competition or playing for reward, but it certainly generated complaints, cheers and loud shouts of disapproval. The noise level was made even higher because of the noise of the dominoes rattling and being banged on the metal tables, which I assume is all part of the fun. Spain is often regarded as one of the noisiest places on the planet, and the playing of dominoes and dice games outside cafes has been banned in Seville, because the intensity of noise disturbs local residents and tourists. I began to see why.

Dominoes may best be described as a game of logic and, like all such games, is important in keeping the brain lively and active. This is particularly important for the elderly. In addition, the act of holding and moving dominoes helps to maintain dexterity and alertness. Although dominoes are a Chinese invention, and were sold by the Chinese equivalent of a friendly Betterware salesman, if you didn't have a set of dominoes in China you were no one. It was to be five hundred years later before they first appeared in Europe, and were brought to Italy in the Eighteenth Century. It is assumed that the game found its way from China to Europe by missionaries who loved playing this Eighteenth Century equivalent of a video game to while away the small hours. The pieces themselves were originally made from ivory, as well as granite, marble, brass or soapstone. Fortunately, most present day dominoes are made from plastic or Bakelite. Judging from the loud noise, I am assuming that Canarian dominoes are made from granite.

I watched the game for a few minutes before moving on. As well as enjoying the game, it was good to see that these elderly men and their friends can meet and enjoy each other's company. We often read distressing stories of the elderly in the UK who are trapped inside their homes for days on end, because of the poor weather and the lack of visitors or any form of companionship, which is so important for all of us. This group of domino players certainly have other ideas.

# A Winter's Tale

I enjoy live theatre of any kind, but rarely get the opportunity since we moved to Spain and the Canary Islands. This is not to say there isn't any culture over here, there is plenty, but it is in Spanish, which can make a new play difficult to follow. Generally, I find it is always best to read the plot before we turn up at the theatre. I still remember the first time that I saw the musical 'Mama Mia' in Spanish whilst visiting Madrid. I was under the impression that the story was about Abba, which left me very confused, as I could not quite see how a Greek Island had entered the plot. Finally, I realised that 'Mama Mia' had very little to do with the Swedish pop group. It really was not a very successful evening, mainly because I didn't have a clue what was going on.

As with many expats, I jump at the opportunity to watch a live performance if it is performed locally, and was not going to miss the opportunity of seeing Shakespeare's Midsummer Night's Dream after so many years, which was presented on the island a few days ago. It did seem a little odd seeing a performance of Shakespeare's 'A Midsummer Night's Dream' in mid December in a theatre surrounded by Christmas trees and decorations. Even more odd was that the performance was going to be in Spanish presented by a group of players in the Canary Islands. Still, as 'A Midsummer Night's Dream' was the first ever Shakespeare play that I saw performed at my school many years ago; it would no doubt bring back many memories.

I am not a great lover of bastardised Shakespeare and arrived at the theatre with a degree of apprehension; after all, the current vogue is to 'modernise' the plays of Shakespeare in order to make them more accessible and appealing to the modern generation. In reality, of course, many interpretations fail miserably to achieve this and tend to put off rather more people than modernisation is supposed to encourage. Admittedly, some attempts have been quite successful, but I also recall a number of embarrassing attempts that have appeared on the big screen. Even so, an enthusiastic Leonardo DiCaprio, did his very best to liven up the plot in the film of Romeo and Juliet, and won the 'Golden Globe' for his efforts.

Many will not agree, but in my view Shakespeare is not for tampering with. This play has been around since about 1590 and may be said to have stood the test of time in its original form. Even though I am well aware that his plays have been translated into most of the World's languages, I did wonder how the story of Bottom and Puck would fare in this particular Midsummer's tale just a couple of weeks before Christmas.

The play was performed 'in the round', of which I am sure Shakespeare would have approved, although I suspect he would have preferred to see an audience that was standing, cheering and jeering, whilst swilling around jugs of mead, to be more worthy of his efforts. No, we were very comfortably seated, in the front row, and the largely Spanish and Canarian audience were unusually quiet, with not a stifled laugh, cough or mobile phone conversation to be heard throughout the auditorium. I think it was best described as respectful silence, or maybe shock at what this ancient English playwright had written.

To be honest, 'A Midsummer Night's Dream' is not an easy play to follow, with four consecutive plots at the same time, which can make it a little confusing. The humour does not lend itself to present day appeal, and a fairy having sex with a 'donkey' may not be in the best possible taste and would certainly lead to present day legal action, if not intervention from the RSPCA. Although the poetry and language is lost for an English speaker, the same timeless magical quality came through in just the same way that I remember from so many years ago.

'A Midsummer Night's Dream' is a strange play in many ways, yet this Canarian interpretation of a play written by a Tudor Englishman over 400 years ago was performed with great enthusiasm. I thoroughly enjoyed it, and it was a performance that I doubt I will ever forget.

## The Language Key

The past often beckons us to ask more searching questions and to apply more challenging thinking to unresolved questions. Advances in archaeological techniques, as well as scientific methods, continually surprise and encourage us to investigate further. One recent discovery in the Canary Islands has provided us with yet another opportunity to reconnect with our past.

It has long been agreed that the first inhabitants of the Canary Islands came from North Africa, the Berbers. Language fragments, as well as genetic research, support this view, yet many mysteries remain. One such mystery is that although the main Canary Islands were inhabited at the time of the European conquest, the islanders had no knowledge of navigation.

Historians continue to ask whether the original inhabitants of the Canary Islands, the Guanches, were brought to the islands by force, or whether they arrived from choice.

'Guanches' is the term generally used to refer to the original inhabitants of all the Canary Islands, although the term originally referred to only the natives of Tenerife. The name 'Majo' is the correct word to use when referring to the aboriginal inhabitants of Fuerteventura and Lanzarote.

These people lived in a 'stone age' state before the European conquest, with no knowledge of metals, although they made pottery, cultivated barley and kept goats, sheep and pigs. The 'Majo' fished and collected wild fruit and vegetables that they could find. They lived in caves or basic stone dwellings. Interestingly, the society was polygamous, with women often having three husbands, which was the consequence of killing female babies to limit the population on an island with very limited resources.

Recently, archaeologists have been investigating inscriptions on a cave wall on the slopes of Tindaya mountain in Fuerteventura, and these could help to translate the written language used by the Majo before the Spanish came to colonise during the 14th and 15th Centuries.

Two alphabets have been identified by archaeologists that seem to represent members of a family as a tree, where one alphabet used is of Berber origin and the other has a Latin origin. A phrase is used in these inscriptions that identifies 'son of Makuran' and this appears to be the language of the inhabitants of the eastern islands of the Canaries where aboriginal Majo lived, and this language has been defined as a lost language of Lanzarote and Fuerteventura.

These early inhabitants tended to live in isolation from each other geographically in the eastern islands, and archaeologists believe that their language originated from 1st Century Libya and Rome.

Inscriptions similar to those found recently have been found at Gholaia in Libya and in other sites in Fuerteventura and Lanzarote, but never before have the two alphabets been discovered and used in parallel.

These archaeologists report that the panel discovered at the Cuchillete de Buenavista site has the wording 'Timamasi Timamasir Avmakuran' that is translated as 'son of Makuran and Timamasi, daughter of Timamasi' in the Latin Libyan version, but as 'W-MKRN' and translated as 'aw makuran or son of Makuran' in Berber Libyan.

This panel may well be the Canarian equivalent of the 'Rosetta Stone', which could unlock many secrets of the ancient language of the eastern Canary Islands that disappeared many years ago. It is a valuable discovery that could assist in much the same way as the Rosetta Stone helped to decipher ancient Egyptian hieroglyphics for the first time when it was discovered in 1799.

## 'Por Favor'

As a child growing up, I was taught what was seen as 'basic good manners'. I was often told to "mind your manners", and thoroughly drilled in the use of "please" and "thank you". If I forgot, or ignored basic courtesy, my parents, or other relatives, quickly reminded me.

This process of being civilised by adults caused me some confusion when I first started to learn Spanish. I remember being warned not to over use the Spanish words 'por favor' (please) when ordering in a cafe bar, or in shops, on the basis that the Spanish rarely use the expression, and when foreigners use it, it is seen as "unacceptably pushy". This comment confused me, and over the years I have made a point of listening to the Spanish ordering food and drink in bars and restaurants, and it is true that very few Spanish use these simple words of courtesy. Their orders are more of a demand than a request, but they mostly say "gracias" afterwards. Don't misunderstand me, most Spanish people are polite; they may smile and add a friendly thank you, but the basic manners of courtesy, as many British people were traditionally taught, are simply not used.

Maybe things are about to change if a recent report is to be believed. One cafe owner, Maria, in Madrid, is so annoyed with many of her Spanish customers whom she regards as rude that she is charging more for coffee and pastries to those customers whom she regards as impolite. Prices may vary from 3 euros for a coffee to 5 euros if customers are deemed to be rude. The price of a cup of good coffee can fall to as low as 1.30 euros if a customer is especially polite. It is the little words of 'please' and 'thank you' that make all the difference, according to Maria.

The idea was inspired by a similar scheme in France, which has been a great success. It is working in Maria's cafe bar too, and Maria reports that already she has seen a change in attitude and politeness to both herself and her staff. Maria blames the pace of everyday life that has become so hectic, and customers simply forget to be polite until it hurts their pockets. Much of this is a cultural issue, of course, and Maria, who is from Columbia, maintains that the Spanish are less inclined to use the words 'please' and 'thank you' than by people in her own country, who Maria sees as more well-mannered.

I can see where Maria is coming from, but I would also like her to consider the option of customers being allowed to pay less for their coffee and croissant if the waiter is rude, does not listen or gets the order wrong. Personally, I am all for good manners, and I am grateful that my parents ensured that I behaved appropriately. I will continue to use 'por favor' when I order my coffee and croissant, but only in moderation.

# Fact, Fiction or What?

The
Canary
Islander

## Irish Monk Discovers New Canary Island - then loses it!

Most people recognise the Canary Islands archipelago as being a cluster of seven inhabited islands. Of course, there are many more islets and rocky outcrops, which few people mention or know anything about. Personally, I regard the archipelago as consisting of eight inhabited islands, and those who have visited the beautiful, yet small island of La Graciosa, just off Lanzarote, will know what I mean. However, this story is about the ninth island, the ghost island, which is still being looked for...

The mysterious island of San Borondón, which is the Canarian name for an Irish monk called Saint Brendan of Clonfert, the Irish patron saint of travellers who lived around 500AD. Brendan was a monk in Tralee, County Kerry, who sailed in a small boat with 14 fellow monks into the Atlantic Ocean, in search of the New World. In true Irish fashion, best retold with a glass or two of Guinness, the story goes that Brendan met with fire hurling demons, a variety of monstrous creatures, and floating crystal columns, which were possibly icebergs; they also rescued three other monks from the inhospitable waters of the Atlantic. Eventually, they landed on an island where they found trees and a great deal of vegetation; it many ways, it was a true Garden of Eden. The monks lived on the island for six years when one day, as they were celebrating mass, the island began to move in the water, described as rather like a whale. After many trials and tribulations, Brendan eventually found his way back to Ireland with many a tale to tell over his glass of mead.

At the time, it was thought that the monks had reached the shores of North America, or possibly other Atlantic islands, such as the Canary Islands. Over time, it was thought that this new island, now named San Borondón', was an island within the Canaries archipelago, somewhere to the west of La Gomera, El Hierro and La Palma. Other sailors attempted to reach it, but when they got close to its shores, the island became covered with mist and vanished.

San Borondón existed in the minds of many people, with detailed accounts from sailors who claimed that they had landed and explored the island before it sank once again into the Atlantic Ocean. Indeed, in some early Atlantic treaties concerning the Canary Islands, there are references to "the islands of Canaria, already discovered or to be discovered", just in case. Indeed, the Island of San Borondón is clearly referred to on several maps of the period.

In the 18th Century, tens of thousands of witnesses declared to the authorities that they had seen the ghostly island from the mountains of El Hierro. Despite further expeditions, the island would not yield its secrets. The persistence of this legend of the voyage of Saint Brendan to the Promised Land of the Saints, the Islands of Happiness and Fortune, remains to this day. It is still possible to talk to some of the residents of El Hierro, La Gomera and La Palma who claim to have seen the island briefly before it sank once again into the brilliant blue waters of the Canary Islands.

*"Let the Guanche drums resound
and the conch shells blow,
for the mysterious island
is appearing in the midst of the waves:
here comes San Borondón,
showing up in the mist
like a queen
with the surf as suite..."*

San Borondón – Cabrera/Santamaria

## Atlantis or What?

I don't have much time for conspiracy theories; I do not believe that Princess Diana was murdered by MI6, nor do I believe that the Moon landing was an elaborate US hoax filmed in Neil Armstrong's back garden. However, I am intrigued by the story of Atlantis, and the links with the Canary Islands that pop up from time to time. This intrigue was fed even more a few days ago following a meeting with a group of divers who were visiting the islands…

Over the years, the tantalising story of the lost city of Atlantis is thought to have been Bermuda, the Azores, Gibraltar, the Bahamas, whilst the Russians claimed to have found it 100 miles off the coast of Cornwall. Boring cynics claim that it only existed in the mind of that wise old bird, Plato, who 2600 years ago was merely giving an example, rather than referring to a literal place on the map. Indeed, somewhere near Greece would seem to be the most likely place of all.

Atlantis was considered to be a major sea power located in the Atlantic Ocean. Its kings were descended from Poseidon, the god of the sea, but their divinity became diluted after mixing with humans. The island conquered much of Africa and Western Europe and by 9600BC had put paid to most of its enemies. Plato describes the island in some detail, with mountains to the north and a plain to the south.

Over the years, scholars have attempted to locate the real Atlantis, believing that it represented some form of ancient superpower, with others claiming that that the destruction of Atlantis was inspired by the Black

Sea floods of around 5000 BC, which might have also inspired the stories of the major flood in the Old Testament.

Plato claimed that Atlantis disappeared "in a single day and night, disappearing in the depths of the sea", after it failed to successfully invade Athens. Tsunamis were recorded in the region, with one massive event hitting Lisbon with a 10-storey tidal wave in 1755. Plato referred to Atlantis in his writings as an island in front of the straits known as 'the pillars of Hercules'; it is likely that these pillars were the Straits of Gibraltar. Plato's detailed description has focussed the search on the Atlantic and Mediterranean as the most likely sites for the city.

It is currently claimed that Atlantis is submerged under mud flats somewhere off the coast of Spain, just off Cadiz to be more exact, according to some scientists. The exact location has been pinpointed with the assistance of digital mapping, radar and underwater technology, using a satellite photo of a suspected submerged city to locate the site. Interestingly, US scientists claim that the residents who survived the destructive tsunami fled and eventually created new cities inland; these cities have been located in marshland and it is evidence from these sites that is being used in the current underwater surveys.

One event that continues to fascinate me is an account of a discovery that appeared online very briefly some months ago. Grid-like lines that resembled city streets were spotted on Google Earth, just off the Canary Islands. Google quickly dismissed the suggestions, claiming that the lines were left by a boat that was collecting data for them. However, this event excited many researchers and the Google explanation was dismissed with some cynicism by some experts. Interestingly, all accounts of this discovery were quickly removed from the Internet, with those in the know claiming no knowledge of the discovery. Indeed, the divers that I have been talking to are investigating these claims more thoroughly. Maybe, just maybe, a conspiracy theory is evolving here…

There are many who continue to claim that Atlantis sank into the Atlantic Ocean, leaving its highest mountains as islands calling from the sea. These islands are, of course, the Canary Islands and that the native people of these islands, the Guanches, were descendants of the people of Atlantis. Whether Atlantis is ever found, if indeed it ever existed, the story of the rise and fall of this great power, is certainly a fascinating and inspirational one, which will continue to be linked with the Canary Islands for many years to come.

## Aliens Visit the Canary Islands Too!

Residents and our regular visitors will already know what makes the Canary Islands special. It seems that it is no longer a well-kept secret, and it could be that aliens are already checking the islands out too, as this account from the 1970s would seem to suggest.

Unidentified Flying Objects or UFOs have always made headline news, but could also be linked to military operations, and would need to be kept secret. However, 40 years ago in the Canary Islands, a UFO was witnessed by thousands of residents across three different islands; the first being on June 22, 1976.

The incident was first reported at 21.27 by all the crew of the ship Atrevida, a Spanish Naval ship near the coast of Fuerteventura.

The crew of the Atrevida described a yellow and blue light that was moving from the island of Fuerteventura towards the ship; the light stopped and hovered in one position. During the following two minutes the yellow and blue light went out, which was followed by a rotating beam.

The crew reported that a halo appeared with yellow and blue light that lasted for around 40 minutes, but the original ball of light was no longer visible.

The captain of the Atrevida described the light as dividing into two parts; a blue cloud from the centre appeared and then vanished, and the upper part began to spiral quickly in an irregular fashion before disappearing.

He also reported that the circular halo was bright enough to light up the nearby areas of land on Fuerteventura and the water surrounding the ship, so that this UFO was thought to be very close to the ship. However, the radar tracking on the ship did not detect any evidence of this sighting.

On the same day, a doctor in Tenerife was travelling by taxi to visit a patient in Las Rosas. When he arrived at the patient's home, he saw a hovering motionless sphere, which he thought was made of a crystalline material and transparent, and that the sphere was electric blue in colour. He also described seeing three control consoles on a metal platform inside the sphere. The doctor described seeing tall images of people wearing some type of head protection and red clothing inside the sphere.

The doctor observed a semi-transparent central tube from the sphere releasing blue smoke, and then the sphere grew to the size of a 20 storey house, rose to a greater height, and made a whistling sound, but the crew and platform remained the same size. By this time, other people in the village had come out of their homes and also witnessed this strange sighting. The doctor described how the UFO then accelerated and moved away at a very fast speed, dissolving into a shape of a spindle that was blue and red underneath, which matched the description given by the captain of the Atrevida off the coast of Fuerteventura, some distance away. The doctor described the formation of a blue halo that had a brilliant light, which matched the comments made by the crew of the Atrevida.

Three days after these sightings, the Spanish Air Force authorised an official investigation into these strange events, and interviewed many of those who had witnessed the appearance of the large glowing light on June 22. This investigation attempted to categorise the witnesses in order to separate what they considered to be reliable witnesses from others described as possibly under the influence of alcohol or drugs, illiterate or mentally challenged and therefore considered to be unreliable. However, the investigator also interviewed aeronautical engineers, pilots and astronomers considered to be reliable.

All the evidence was collected that included photographs of the sphere, illustrations, drawings and accounts from witnesses. This investigation eventually reported that there were no military exercises operating on the date of the sightings of this sphere or other aerial traffic that could explain this unusual occurrence, and reported that witnesses had observed an unidentified aerial phenomenon on 22 June 1976.

Gran Canaria was also the destination for this UFO in November 1976, when it was sighted again personally by the Commanding General of Spain's Air Force Canary Islands Air Zone whilst flying in a transport aircraft. Air force personnel at the air base and crew on board another naval ship docked at the air base harbour also reported seeing this UFO.

Again, a large halo followed this UFO appearance at the air base on Gran Canaria, which was the same pattern as seen in June that year in Fuerteventura and Tenerife.

This incident was also investigated by the Spanish Air Force and the report that was later published said that this was clearly a craft of unknown origin, and propelled by an unknown energy and was moving freely over the skies of the Canary Islands.

Over the years, these incidents seem to have been quietly forgotten, but there are still those who recount this story as vividly as the day that these incidents took place. Whether these incidents were linked to some kind of secret military exercise, or some kind of visit from another world, remains a mystery, but it might be worth carefully checking who is sitting next to you on the beach.

# The Big Time Mix Up

Expats living in Spain often have to remind themselves that Spain currently has two time zones, as well as observing daylight saving time. In Peninsular Spain, the Balearic Islands, Melilla and Ceuta, Central European Time is observed, whilst the Canary Islands observe Greenwich Mean Time (also known as Western European Time), which is the same as the UK.

Since Central European Time is one hour ahead of that in the UK, it can sometimes be a little awkward when calling friends and relatives or indeed phoning the bank or businesses in the UK. In the Canary Islands, which use Greenwich Mean Time, we can easily call businesses, relatives and friends in the UK since we are in the same time zone, but it can cause problems when trying to call anyone in Madrid close to siesta time.

There is currently a movement in Spain, supported by many prominent businesses, suggesting that Spain moves its time zone from Central European Time to Western European Time, which is its natural time zone. Many people do not realise that Spain has been in the wrong time zone for decades. During World War Two, it was the Spanish dictator, General Franco, who decided that Spain should be in the same time zone as Nazi Germany during a meeting in Hitler's railway carriage on the Spanish border on 23 October 1940.

The Nazis had already occupied France, Holland, Belgium and Norway, and Italy had joined forces with Hitler. Hitler wanted Spain's support, and since the country was in turmoil after its own Civil War, Franco wanted to be seen as staying neutral, but as a gesture of support to the Nazis switched Spanish time to be one hour ahead and in line with Nazi Germany, where it has remained ever since.

A number of prominent economists debate that remaining in the current time zone has a negative effect upon productivity, as well as the country's birth rate. Although Spain is geographically in line with Morocco, Portugal and the UK, its clocks remain in the same time line with countries in Eastern Europe, such as Hungary and Poland. This means that the sun rises and sets later when compared to other countries in the region. As a result, Spaniards sleep for around 53 minutes less than other Europeans; they work longer hours, but at lower levels of productivity.

This time zone shift plays a role in the country's relatively unusual daily schedule with late meals and sleep times. The Spanish are well known for late nights, since the sun rises and sets much later than in the rest of its time zone. Since there is a break at midday for a big lunch and siesta for two or three hours, workers rarely finish work before 8.00pm or 9.00pm, which leaves little time for personal and family life. Indeed, this is seen as one of the reasons why Spain currently has such a low birth rate – there just isn't enough time!

Spain has already aligned some of its working practices, such as shortening long holiday weekends, with the rest of Europe, but many doubt that Spanish culture will adapt quite so quickly to a change in the time zone. The getting up late and going to bed late culture will take considerable time to adjust. The siesta, for instance, is one example of a cultural practice that has nothing to do with Franco's change in the time zone. Before air conditioning became commonplace, the siesta was a way of getting through long, hot afternoons. Many Spanish people continue to have two jobs; one before and one after the siesta period. It is a way of life that could prove resistant to political change, however well intentioned.

Many regard the continuance of Franco's time zone as the late dictator's final insult, which needs to be changed even though it has become a way of life.

## Fuerteventura and the Nazis

The Canary Island of Fuerteventura is usually associated with beautiful beaches, breath-taking scenery and plenty of wind to indulge in some of those energetic water sports. The island is also particularly popular with German and British tourists, but very little is known or discussed about the darker side of Fuerteventura's history, involving Nazi Germany. This is the story of Villa Winter, and during my recent visit to the island, I had the opportunity to meet with and discuss aspects of the story with several local people who know the property and history well.

Villa Winter is an impressive, mysterious and very large building situated close to the village of Cofete, on the Jandia peninsular. The villa was built in a remote spot, and is accessible only on a dust track by heavy duty 4-wheel drive vehicles. Villa Winter belonged to Gustav Winter, who was a German engineer born in Germany's Black Forest in 1893. It is thought that the villa was built in 1937, although official records appear to have been modified to 1946, for reasons that will become apparent later in this story. The villa has two floors, with a tower in the north western part of the property, and a balcony at the front.

Since 1915, Gustav Winter worked for Spain on projects in Gran Canaria and Fuerteventura. In 1937, he signed a lease for the Jandia peninsular from the Conde de Santa Coloma, based in Lanzarote. That same year, Winter left the island for Germany, in order to seek funding. In 1939, local people were barred from the peninsular, which was declared a military zone, due to agreements between General Franco and Adolf Hitler.

The road to the villa, as well as the villa itself, were built by prisoners of war from the concentration camp at Tefia, which later became the island's airport. The building has vast, dark cellars and caves stretching beneath it, and includes a large tower that looks out to sea. It is often suggested that it was built to act as a watch tower for sightings of possible aircraft landings at the nearby airfield of Jandia, as well as a beacon for submarines. Intriguingly, the tower still contains evidence of an enormous fuse box indicating that large and power hungry equipment was used in the tower.

There is well documented evidence of submarines sited around the Canary Islands during the Second World War, and between March and July 1941 submarines visited the harbour of Las Palmas de Gran Canaria a number of times. There continues to be speculation that Fuerteventura was the home of a submarine base, and there are reports of two tunnels built under the mountains, dug into the lava tunnels of an extinct volcano that were used for U boats. Some say that there are still two complete submarines in it, which are claimed to have sunk. This suggestion was investigated by a team of experts from Austria and Spain in the 1970s, yet they lost their lives when their boat exploded during the investigation and their work remains unconfirmed.

There are many stories about Villa Winter, but one common theme is that its role was a safe house for the

Nazis. At the end of the war, it is thought by many that a number of Nazi leaders, including Adolf Hitler, arrived on the island, where plastic surgery was undertaken to change their identities before they escaped to South America, and with Argentina being a favoured destination, since Peron was a friend and ally of Hitler.

We have been told for many years that Hitler and his wife, Eva Braun, committed suicide in an underground bunker in April 1945. According to accounts and propaganda at the time, their bodies were then taken outside and burned by loyal staff before being deposited in a shallow grave. Many experts now believe the story to be untrue and was concocted between the Allies at the end of the war. It is suggested that Hitler travelled from Germany to Fuerteventura where a U boat was waiting to take him to Argentina where he ended his days.

In 1971, Gustav Winter died on the neighbouring island of Gran Canaria. Both he and his widow denied the many stories surrounding the mysterious Villa Winter until their deaths. A distant relative of Gustav Winter attempted to turn the villa into a wellness centre some years ago, but the plans failed. The villa is currently owned by a Spanish building company and will probably be eventually converted into a hotel or restaurant.

Whatever the truth is behind this mysterious building, there remain many unsolved mysteries and speculation surrounding Villa Winter, and many inconsistencies and secrecy remain.

## Promises, Promises

As much as I love the Canary Islands, one of the issues that continues to irritate me are the regular 'grand announcements' by local municipalities and the Islands' Government to a believing public about projects that usually never happen. Things are never quite what they may at first seem.

I can quote a number of relevant examples, but in the last few years there has been much talk about an island railway running from Las Palmas in the north of the island to Puerto Mogan in the south. This is not a vanity project, but a much needed facility for tourists and residents alike. It has created much excitement on the island, a prototype carriage and train were available for public inspection, plans for the track were drawn up, financing agreed, with work due to start on the track and stations in 2014. So far, to the best of my knowledge, 'nada', nothing, not a single track in sight. So what was all that about?

Then there was much excitement about a well-known, national department store that was about to build a new store in the south of the island. This was generally well received, and particularly by the resident Brit population. I recall speaking to very excited staff in their current location who were convinced that the first concrete block was about to be laid, and that they would be offered the opportunity of some of the new jobs that would be created at the store. Has anything happened? No, of course not.

There was also much speculation about a new 'Chinese Village', which was about to be built somewhere in Telde near the fire station and a hardware supermarket. The purpose of this particular project was always a little of a mystery, but I gather that it has something to do with a rather nice hotel being built, together with some lovely gardens in Chinese style. Planning permission was said to have been given and finance agreed. Has anything happened to further this project? No, of course not.

The highlight of my reporting year came when it was announced that a space station would be built at the current airport; this would be designed to propel visitors, with stomachs made of iron, into space for a jolly canapé and a glass or two of bubbly to celebrate their bravery in parting with several thousand euros. There was much celebration at the news, which was billed as the only space facility in Europe for tourists. Many observers thought that the news was a joke for April 1st, but a press conference was called, and the smart suits and frocks were out with a vengeance. Has anything happened? No, of course not. However, in its defence, there was a tragic accident at a similar site in the US involving Virgin Galactica, which I guess hardly sold the experience.

Over the years as a reporter, I have spent hours of time at press conferences and discussions, with the great and the good announcing their latest projects with much aplomb, and usually with impressive, expensive screen presentations. We are told, as usual, about the huge financial and commercial benefits that such projects will bring to the island and its fragile economy, whilst we all know that very little of it will trickle into the pockets of Canarian families, but will be sucked into bottomless corporate pockets overseas. Maybe diversifying from growing tomatoes and bananas is not such a good idea?

So, my plea to the municipalities and the Islands' Government is not to announce such lofty projects until they are quite sure that they are properly funded, agreed and stand a good chance of happening, otherwise it can all look rather silly. It is a little like offering a small child a tasty ice cream, with a chocolate flake, and then flushing it down the loo before the first bite. Cynics will also be well aware that such announcements are usually made just before an election, and so I am anxiously awaiting the next flurry of meaningless announcements before December's General Election. I am sure that many leading these unfilled projects will claim that the World recession and budget cuts have forced them to abandon costly schemes, although I should point out that the projects that I have quoted were announced following the financial crash, so it is unlikely that delays and cancellations can be blamed upon the recession.

With high unemployment, particularly for the youth of the island, these major projects could have provided employment and purpose for many. Were these real projects in the first place, I wonder? Well, I hear that building the promised new Water Park, which is billed as the largest water park in Europe, is shortly due to commence. Maybe this will open and reach fulfilment. I look forward to being proved wrong.

# Keeping it Quirky

The Canary Islander

## The Story of the Smart Pole

Before readers become too excited, I should begin by saying that this 'Letter from the Atlantic' has absolutely nothing to do with a very unfortunate experience that I had as a reporter covering a "story of interest" in a pole dancing bar in the Costa Blanca. Sadly, the Velcro strap on my camera bag had an incident with a pole dancer and her pole whilst she was demonstrating her wide ranging and imaginative skills on a pole that she was clearly very fond of. I will leave this to your imagination, which could be a story for another time.

The 'smart poles' that I am referring to are a new initiative by the local emergency services in the Canary Islands, 112 Canarias, in response to the tragic loss of life by drowning experienced by a number of British holidaymakers visiting these beautiful islands. During the summer of 2014, more than 28 per cent of deaths from beach drownings were linked to British holidaymakers. Sadly, this grim statistic provides the Canary Islands with one of the highest growing drowning incident rates in Spain.

The Canary Government's 112 Emergency Service, which is also known as FRESS, has recently installed the first 'Help Point' on Playa del Ingles beach in Gran Canaria. Essentially, it is a device connected to the emergency services, which provides help in four languages, together with a video conferencing facility to enable the caller to explain the nature of the emergency, as well as providing a messaging facility for the hard of hearing. In many ways, it is the present day equivalent of the UK's blue police boxes from many years ago.

In reality, these 'Help Points' are not really poles, but rather a strange looking exotic variety of mushroom that has popped up outside the Red Cross office and police station in front of the beach. One may wonder why it is not easier to run into the police station or the Red Cross office in an emergency rather than negotiating the pole, but I guess this gadget will come into its own when these offices are closed. The pole would certainly be very useful on more remote beaches that do not have emergency services nearby.

It is hoped that these distinctive poles will eventually be seen across the Canary Islands, and particularly in those areas where bathers are most vulnerable. The video link feature is particularly useful as it will assist both caller and call handler to determine the nature of the emergency more effectively.

Of course, these tragic statistics leaves one to wonder why it is the British who are in the lead on this grim table of death. How many of these incidents were drug and drink related, or were they simply the result of carelessness or ignoring warning signs and flags that appear on most of the popular beaches? It is important for visitors to remember that the Canary Islands are not surrounded by a warm and calm Mediterranean Sea, but the Atlantic Ocean, which is renowned for being both erratic and unforgiving in temperament.

Sudden changes in sea activity can make beach swimming unsafe and lead to tragic accidents.

Whether visiting the Canary Islands or the Costa Blanca, the safety of beach swimming should never be taken for granted, and it is important that everyone is aware of sea and weather conditions, as well as following guidance given by warning notices and flags. Although it is never possible to prevent all accidents, a closer examination of why so many British holidaymakers, in particular, are drowned in such tragic circumstances must surely be a priority.

## It's the Wrong Kind of Sunshine!

UK rail passengers vented their anger last week when they were told that strong sunlight was causing trains to be delayed in Lewisham. It seems that the angle of the sun at this time of the year causes difficulties for the driver being able to see. Frustrated rail passengers were unimpressed by the explanation, described by many as, "The weakest excuse ever", following a catalogue of excuses from the UK train companies, which includes trains being cancelled or delayed due to "leaves on the line", "sun causing tracks to buckle", "snow on the track" and even the "wrong type of rain". According to a spokesman for the train company, the morning glare made it impossible for drivers to see the full length of their train in their mirrors before leaving the station. Might I suggest that they employ a guard?

Following an incident yesterday, I now have some sympathy with this excuse. In the Canary Islands we have sunshine throughout the year and the sun is rarely used as an excuse for closing things down, unless it gets too hot, of course. Even so, it seems that the angle of the sun is also an issue for us here, with the sun's glare making it difficult to drive at this time of the year.

I was driving home through the Canarian town of Vecindario when I finally had to pull in and stop the car for some time, because the sun's glare had become too strong for me to drive safely. Even though I was wearing sunglasses, and the car's sun visor was down, it became impossible to see the road ahead. As it was a busy area, the safest thing to do was to stop and listen to some music until the angle of the sun had changed. It only caused a delay of a few minutes and so was not an issue of concern. However, as it was not an issue that I had faced before, I spoke to several friends who have experienced the same problem, and they agreed that this is something that they often have to deal with at this time of the year.

I really must get a pair of polarising glasses from the Chinese Shop, which I assume will help to overcome the problem, and maybe these could be issued to train drivers too? I am also wondering how train drivers in Norway and Sweden cope with the winter sun there?

So despite the amusement and anger that this issue has caused for the good people of Lewisham, I now have some sympathy with the predicament that the train company faced. Better to be safe than sorry!

## The Booze Cruise

Over the last two years there has been a worrying increase in the number of passengers creating a major disturbance on planes flying to the Canary Islands, as well as on other routes to Spain's sunshine holiday destinations. The most common issue is excessive consumption of alcohol before and during the flight, leading to a number of major incidents. In some cases, offending passengers have had to be restrained during the flight, whilst others have forced pilots to seek a premature landing at another airport, involving delays, inconvenience, distress and increased expenses for the airline and other passengers. Neither is this an entirely British condition, since I am also aware of several Scandinavian airlines that have had similar problems in recent months.

There are now pleasing signs that some airlines are toughening up on their policy towards offending passengers, yet the issue seems to be getting worse. In most cases, these passengers are arrested, fined and often banned from flying on commercial airlines for a number of years. This is to be welcomed, but the penalties are currently clearly not high enough, and I remain unconvinced that the problem is being dealt with effectively and aggressively at source.

Flying is not a pleasurable experience for most people, and many holidaymakers like to have an alcoholic drink to help them relax before they take to the skies. Flights can also be incredibly boring, unless engrossed in a good book, watching a thrilling film on a personal tablet, or able to sleep for a few hours. On-board snacks and drinks do help to relieve some of the boredom. The problem appears to be that some of the cheaper carriers are so desperate to promote their sales of booze and food on board to increase their profit margins, but forget that this actually affects passengers in a way that could create devastating circumstances for the entire flight.

I recall a flight that I took from the UK to Gran Canaria some months ago with a low cost airline; it was an experience that I will never forget, and for all the wrong reasons. The troubles began as soon as a group of wildly excited young men boarded the flight, clearly intoxicated and in the party mood at ten o'clock in the morning. Whether they were intoxicated with booze or drugs, I cannot be certain, but it did not take an expert to recognise that these passengers should never have been allowed to board the plane.

The problems were compounded by the airline's trolley service, which continually plied its trade up and down the aisles every 30 minutes or so on the four-hour flight. The group of young men were sold beers and spirits in abundance leading to even more riotous, noisy and foul mouthed behaviour. Instead of refusing them more alcohol, they were encouraged to drink more, and I lost count of the number of fifty-pound notes that changed hands on the flight. This group of young men were clearly good customers and would no doubt considerably boost the airline's profit and the cabin crew's commissions.

Meanwhile, myself and other passengers were suffering from the actions of this group of thoughtless partygoers. As well as noisy, foul mouthed, riotous behaviour, we were sprayed and showered with the remaining dregs inside cans of beers, gins and tonics, although the cabin crew were kind enough to offer us moist tissues to mop ourselves with. Finally, one member of the group vomited, partly into a paper bag, with the remainder hitting a passenger seated in the next aisle. We all had to endue the foul stench for the remainder of the journey.

As well as passengers taking greater responsibility for themselves and their own behaviour, airlines and airports clearly need to monitor those attempting to board aircraft in an intoxicated state. As well as enhanced security measures, airlines and airports should adopt a more responsible approach to sales of alcohol on flights. I also question whether it is really necessary to serve alcohol in airports and on aircraft anyway, other than to boost profits? I guess that is my answer; without selling alcohol, ticket prices would rise. After my experience, this is certainly my preferred option.

# Living in Caves

The main news item this week in the Canary Islands has been a tragic case of a 27-year-old German expat, living on the beautiful Island of La Palma who, allegedly, set fire to his own used-toilet paper after relieving himself 'au natural' off a forest trail in a protected natural park. As a result, he set fire to a large, ancient and ecologically valuable pine woodland, causing the death of a fire fighter, who was a park ranger with five children, and was responsible for 2500 people having to be evacuated from their homes. It is also suggested that alcohol or drugs may have played a part in this ongoing tragedy.

According to the suspect, after he had defecated, he lit the toilet paper, and then sparks leapt from the burning tissue onto dry vegetation, which quickly turned into a vicious fire with devastating consequences. With temperatures approaching 40 degrees, as well as strong winds, the fire quickly got out of control, and approached the island's busiest tourist area, Fuencaliente.

La Palma is the fifth largest of the islands, and is popular because of its protected parks and forests. Dozens of helicopters and planes from other islands were brought to La Palma to assist, as well as 350 fire fighters who, at the time of writing, are still trying to extinguish the blaze. The suspect is currently being held by police, without bail.

According to local sources, the man lives in a cave in this beautiful forested area. Many people still live in caves on several of the Canary Islands. These are not ordinary caves, as one would first imagine, but are often very tastefully converted dwellings, offering all modern conveniences, but in this case, clearly without a toilet. Several that I have been invited to consist of several interconnected rooms, have water, electricity, Internet connection and even air conditioning. I have even visited two cave homes that have a sauna, as well as a hot tub; it is hardly rough living. The caves offer remarkably sensible accommodation for modern island living in the Canary Islands, since they remain cool in summer and warm in winter. The early settlers in the Canary Islands, the Guanches, were certainly no fools and knew exactly what they were doing when it came to cave dwelling.

Sadly, many of these caves are now often rented or sold to the trendy expat; those with money, but often with very little accompanying common sense. I am not referring to this particular criminal case, but I have heard a number of reports where these caves are bought up by foreigners as holiday homes, but who have little or no sensitivity to the uniqueness of the Canary Islands and its protected areas. 'Boutique Caves' as they are sometimes called are even sometimes available as rental accommodation, or discovered by the 'beautiful people' and occasional hippies who happen to find one that is abandoned or in a less than liveable state.

Questions are rightly now being asked by local people about whether it is acceptable to sell or let these unique dwellings to holidaymakers and expats. Cave and other homes that are situated in high risk and environmentally important areas may need to be especially protected. Yes, it does enhance the rural economy and bring in much needed tourist euros to these areas, but one wonders if the cost to human life, as well as the overall environment, is worth the risk?

As for the German tourist; maybe he should consider using a chemical toilet in future.

## Hug a Tree

Since we moved to a relatively dry and arid part of the Canary Islands, I have come to appreciate the natural beauty of plants and trees now even more than when I lived in the UK. On rare occasions, our neighbour decides to mow his tiny patch of grass, which is the size of a tablecloth; it is so small it takes only a couple of minutes to mow with a strimmer, and I deeply inhale the smell of newly mown grass, which takes me back to the large lawn at our Dorset cottage garden that I used to curse during its weekly mowing. I now miss National Trust gardens, garden centres, complete with garden accessories, greetings cards and cream teas, as well as the variety, freshness and colour of British woodland in spring.

Although there are exceptions, it seems to me that very few Canarians or Spanish appreciate plants, trees and gardens. At every opportunity, their first inclination is to concrete over any remaining patch of soil that they see, or at least cover it with patio tiles. Occasionally, containers are purchased to stand on patios, beautiful plants are purchased, only to wither and die a few days later, because no one can be bothered to water them.

One of our neighbours was horrified when he saw me installing an underground watering system in the garden of our new home a few years ago. He shook his head, and commented that it would cost a lot of money to pay for the water, but in my opinion it is worth every cent. After all, I am a Brit, and I could not exist happily without plants around me.

Even though the locals treat most plants and trees with disdain, Gran Canaria, the island where I live, can boast the most amazing and beautiful botanical garden, Jardin Botanico Canario, near Las Palmas, which is always open to the general public. My partner and I have visited the garden many times, and are usually the only visitors. I doubt that many locals, or indeed tourists, know of its existence, or can be bothered to visit, but it is certainly one of the many treasures of this island.

I used to enjoy looking at the trees that run through the centre of our village. They are all the same, and can look untidy for part of the year. Birds and cicadas enjoy sitting on them and it is good to see greenery where otherwise there would be the usual concrete and tiles. Each year, Town Hall staff trim them, which can be amusing. Sometimes the trimming takes the form of cuboids or maybe pyramids - we never really know quite what to expect, but nature takes its course and they eventually resume their natural shape.

Several months ago, contractors arrived in our village to give the trees their annual trim. A few days later, I was horrified to see that the pruning had been total. Hardly a leaf or branch had been left in place and only a grey stump remained. Over the last few months I have checked, and it looks as if all the trees are dead. Several locals nod knowledgeably and assure me that this form of brutal pruning is necessary every few years, and that they will return to their former glory. Others shake their head and tell me that they are dead, but why does it matter? They are only trees after all...

My hope is that the trees, once they have recovered from their shock, and Mother Nature does her stuff, will all suddenly spring into life once again, and send their shoots out with a vengeance. I will be keeping a close eye on them.

# Chinese Takeaway

A story about a Chinese tourist visiting Germany made interesting reading this week. In many ways, it is a sad story, but the innocence and bewilderment expressed are very similar to situations that many of us find ourselves in when living as newly arrived expats in a country where the rules, customs and language are not clearly understood.

The Chinese tourist had his wallet stolen and so, sensibly, went to the police station to report his loss. Sadly, he did not enter the police station, but instead found himself in the Town Hall where he inadvertently signed an application form claiming refugee status, handed over his passport, which led him into a bewildering nightmare of official German bureaucracy - stranding him as a refugee in an asylum centre for 12 days.

Instead of enjoying the delights that German tourism has to offer in a pleasant hotel, the man spent 12 nights on a less than comfortable camp bed in an asylum centre. Although he was well treated and given food and spending money like other refugees, he was also fingerprinted, given a medical examination and taken over 200 kilometres from where he had planned to spend his holiday. Staff at the reception centre were puzzled, since the man was so well dressed, and kept asking for his passport, which was uncharacteristic of asylum seekers.

Eventually, the staff realised that something was badly wrong and called in help from the local Chinese takeaway, as well as using a translation app on a mobile phone. Finally, they released their visitor and he continued his travels to France and Italy, no doubt relieved that his German 'holiday' was over.

This story reminds me of a number of emails that I regularly receive from British expats who find themselves in trouble with the Spanish authorities, simply because they do not understand the customs, or documents that they are asked to sign. I often hear British expats complaining about what they perceive as "burdensome Spanish bureaucracy". Of course, in reality, expats living in the UK comment about exactly the same problem with the British system, as do expats living in Germany, France and Italy. The problem is rarely to do with bureaucracy, but is more than likely to be combined with issues relating to a poor understanding of local customs, laws and language.

When moving to Spain or any other European country, expats face a bewildering array of legal paperwork. In haste, and to swiftly move on with our business, we often sign things that we should not without first asking questions and seeking clarification. Many do sign, trusting that the bank, town hall, traffic or police authorities will have their best interests at heart, but this is not always the case. Even if you have taken the trouble to learn Spanish, it is always wise to have documents checked by a lawyer, gestor, or someone who really does understand what you are signing, before you sign on the dotted line.

Even if we do speak the language, I have always maintained that in matters relating to health, finance and the law, it is better to seek clarification in our own native language. Yes, it may cost a little more, but this disappears into insignificance in circumstances where you may lose your home, face a criminal charge or severe financial penalties. I suspect that the Chinese visitor will be much more careful about what he signs in future.

# The Financial and Legal Expat

## A New Banking Experience for Expats

Many of us are not too keen on banks at the moment, and particularly since the recession. I know of many expats who find banking in Spain a trial that has to be endured. Long queues, indifferent service, as well as high charges often make the Spanish banking experience unappealing, and with little attention to the needs of their customers. Both banks that used to operate in the village where I live have closed their branches, leaving many villagers who do not own a car with little choice, but to use the infrequent bus service to the nearest town. There is good news on the horizon, and I suspect that things will change for the better in the not too distant future.

New banks are springing up in many countries. These are app based banks that operate using a smartphone and the Internet. They have no branches and no reams of paperwork to sign. They offer a basic current banking account operated from a distance. They issue a debit card that can be used in cash dispensers in all countries and, best of all, there are no charges.

With Brexit, the new reality for expats is that banking facilities operating throughout Europe may become even more difficult. Most, if not all, British banks are now refusing to open accounts for expats with addresses outside the UK. I have received a number of complaints from expats living in Greece who are finding that difficulties with the Greek banking system are forcing them to seek alternatives in order to reliably receive their British pensions. Sadly, offshore accounts now seem to be the only alternative, since British High Street banks no longer wish to help.

There are several newcomers to the world of expat banking operating through the use of apps on iPhones and Android smartphones, one of which may help to solve some of these issues for expats. 'Monese' is a bank that offers a new approach to banking with an emphasis upon providing international low cost banking facilities for expats from all countries, which may help to overcome the increasingly restrictive banking services across Europe.

Expats can open an account in under three minutes (which is true, because I tried it a few days ago); users must have a government based ID document, such as a passport to use the app. Customers can use their overseas address and usual mobile phone number without difficulty. The bank charges a monthly fee, and in return customers receive a Visa debit card to use in local shops, as well as to withdraw cash in their local currency from most ATMs. Full banking facilities, such as direct debits, standing orders, pension credits and all that you would expect from a traditional High Street bank are provided, but without the hassle.

The account opening process is in English, which has made the entire procedure a pleasant and trouble free experience. The bank's app and webpages are well designed, work smoothly and are in English. One other advantage is that I was not deluged with paper, as the only physical item being the debit card that was posted to me; the bank certainly lives up to its 'green' credentials. So far, I am impressed and this is by far the easiest way to open and operate a British based bank account. Give it a try; I suspect that you will like it.

A similar account, currently operating in euros only, is offered by 'N26', an app based bank in Germany and regulated and protected by the German Bundesbank, which is the broad equivalent of the UK's financial regulatory authority. The opening process took exactly eight minutes by video call from my smartphone to confirm my identity. A very helpful lady took me through the process; they took a photo of my passport and me. A few days later, a MasterCard debit card arrived though the post, which I can use in Spain and the Canary Islands, as well as worldwide in the usual way, and there are no charges for drawing out cash from cash dispensers either.

Similar app based banks are currently being launched in the UK. I particularly wanted a bank that operated in pounds and euros, as well as being protected by a state regulatory authority. The banks that I have mentioned, as with other new start up banks, intend to offer joint accounts, credit cards, deposit and savings accounts, loans and overdrafts, insurance and other services once their basic service is established.

My new accounts can be used to make payments by direct debit, receive funds as well as processing all the other transactions that I currently make from my Spanish bank account. Being a cautious Brit when it comes to legal and financial matters, I am going to use the account for shopping and cash withdrawals, before I plunge headlong into completely transferring my account. However, these early days tell me that queuing in a bank branch waiting to see if someone can be bothered to attend to me are long gone. Gone too are the endless sheets of meaningless paper. Welcome to the new banking experience!

For further information and links to some of these new banks, please go to the Expat Survival section of my website: http://expat.barriemahoney.com

## Holiday Health Insurance

I am often asked, "Will I need health insurance in the Canary Islands?" to which my answer is always, "Yes, of course". This is usually followed by a comment that "I have the European Health Card, surely that will cover me?"

In theory, the answer is that it should, but in reality, it rarely does. To be clear, the European Health Card is mainly intended for an emergency, such as a life and death situation when emergency treatment is required. It is not intended to deal with existing conditions, minor ailments, sunburn and too much booze, which are often the main complaints. If you are taken ill on holiday, there is a good chance that the hotel or holiday complex will call a private ambulance and not one from the National Health Service. The reason is simple; the hotel will receive a commission on your misfortune. The private ambulance will, in turn, take you to a private hospital. Again the reason is simple; the ambulance company will receive a commission from the hospital. Yes, you will probably receive very good treatment, but only after your credit card has been debited with a large deposit, and a larger bill to follow.

Some time ago, I was waiting at the check-in desk of one of the private hospitals on the island. At my side was a distraught holidaymaker, Adrian, from the UK who was trying to get his wife, Ellen, admitted to the hospital for emergency treatment. Ellen had a collapsed lung and was waiting in the private ambulance outside. The hospital refused Adrian's European Health Card, and it was only when Adrian agreed to a 3000 euros debit from his credit card as a 'deposit', would they agree to admit Ellen into the hospital for treatment, despite Ellen being in considerable pain, and having difficulty in breathing without assistance. To add insult to injury, before the ambulance staff would agree to release Ellen from the ambulance, Adrian had to pay a substantial fee for their service.

Later, I met up with Adrian who was waiting outside the hospital. He looked pale and was clearly very anxious. I asked him if I could help and he told me that they were due to leave for home the following day and that the hospital had told him that Ellen would not be fit to travel for some time, and only after a number of expensive tests and procedures had been completed. Adrian did not have enough funds to pay the hospital bills, nor would he have any accommodation for himself the following day. Adrian would have to call friends and family in the UK to ask for money to be sent out to help him until his wife could travel home. He had no mobile phone and so I let him use mine.

It was a desperate situation that I have heard many times before. Adrian and Ellen had booked a last minute, cheap, package holiday, but had decided not to buy the optional travel and health insurance, because they already had a European Health Card. In these circumstances, the card would be of no use, unless they could negotiate with the hospital for Ellen's transfer to the National Health Hospital, which in my experience rarely takes place following admission to a private hospital. Either way, Adrian and Ellen would have a huge financial problem to deal with upon their return home.

I have just heard of another very sad story of a holidaymaker who died upon arrival at one of the islands. Again, the couple had no insurance, nor means of paying to get the body home, which alone would cost around 7000 euros. I understand that generous friends and family are currently trying to raise funds in the UK to assist the widow. At times of sickness and bereavement, worry about money should be of the least concern.

Finally, do be careful of those private hospitals that advertise acceptance of the European Health Card. They may do, but not for all conditions and not in all circumstances. My best advice is always to take out health and travel insurance before you come on holiday, or bring a credit card with a very large credit limit, just in case.

## Customs Confusion

I've had a long running battle with the Aduana, the customs people, over here for many years. Despite various explanations of their purpose in life, I have never really understood the logic of how this faceless bureaucracy operates, if indeed any logic is used. My detest and distrust of this all-powerful organisation came originally from ordering a simple cable from eBay for my computer, which could not be purchased on the islands. The total cost was around four pounds, which included postage, for which the Aduana decided to add a few cents for IGIC (the Canary Islands' equivalent of VAT) together with a handling charge of around 15 euros, as well as IGIC on top of their 'service charge'. Like a fool, on this occasion, I paid up, as I desperately needed the cable. My letter of complaint fell on deaf ears and I heard no more.

Don't misunderstand me, I have no objection to paying my fair share of taxes; indeed, they are fundamental to the operation of any civilised society. As the recent Google tax scandal has shown, people get terribly upset when taxes appear to be unfair and seem to favour one particular group of the population or major multinational companies at the expense of ordinary people. Taxes need to be fair and transparent to be effective.

Over the years I have had several bad experiences with the Aduana, often resulting in me refusing to accept delivery, which I hate doing as we have a very nice postman, who I do not like upsetting. My mother's words of "cutting off one's nose to spite one's face" also spring to mind on some occasions when I have rejected a delivery. However, I do object to being taken for a ride over something that is clearly not fair.

As an expat living on these islands, I know that many of us rely on companies, such as eBay and Amazon, to purchase items that we cannot find locally. Speaking to Canarian and Spanish residents, it appears that this tax is often applied more to expats than the local population, although I cannot prove this.

Many expats have become resigned to having to pay a hefty surcharge on Christmas gifts kindly sent by relatives and friends in the UK. Even the odd DVD and small gift tends to have the postman knocking at the door for a contribution to the Aduana fund. Worst still are the large courier companies whose standard 'service charges' can be eye watering for simply collecting a few euros of tax for the Aduana, as well as being responsible for severe delays as items are held up in Madrid whilst phone calls are made and the required paperwork is produced. What a waste of time and energy!

I mentioned earlier that the system is illogical. Several months ago, I ordered a camera from Amazon in the UK. It cost over 400 pounds, and in true Amazon tradition I was delighted to discover that the 20 per cent UK VAT was taken off the invoice before I paid, since I live outside the EU for tax purposes. It is then both understandable and acceptable to pay tax in the Canary Islands of 7 per cent upon delivery, which I was fully expecting. Surprisingly, in this case, my new camera was delivered tax free, without even a murmur of a request for tax or a service charge levy. Maybe I was just lucky on this occasion.

Now for the good news; the Canary Islands' Government is currently considering raising the minimum value of postal items for tax purposes from 22 euros to 150 euros. This proposed change would mean that residents of the Canary Islands would be able to make purchases online that have the same conditions as other people within the EU. Let us hope that common sense finally prevails.

## No More UK Banking for Expats

It used to be so easy. Not so many years ago, UK expats would simply call into the local branch of their UK bank, tell them that they were going to move to another country, give their new address, and that would be that. Banking would continue as normal, but with bank statements and correspondence popping into the letterbox of their new home overseas.

A few years later, it became more difficult for UK expats to maintain a personal loan or a UK credit card once they moved abroad. A few years on, and hot on the heels of the banking crisis, new security measures and a paranoid fear of potential terrorist money laundering, it is now almost impossible for expats to open any form of bank account with a UK high street bank.

I received an email from Joyce, who lives in the Costa Blanca, last week. She is a newly arrived expat, and very excited about her new home in the sun. Joyce and her partner Mike have worked hard over the years to finally achieve their dream. She has banked with the same UK high street bank since she was a teenager, has never had an overdraft, and maintains a substantial deposit with the bank. Following the sale of their home in the UK, she called into her local bank branch to tell them that she was moving to Spain, and tried to give them her new address.

Joyce was horrified at the bank's reaction, which was not as expected; the bank immediately cancelled her credit card and told her that they would be unable to maintain an account for her whilst her main home was in Spain. The bank suggested that she transfer her account to their offshore subsidiary, which Joyce is reluctant to do, since with all the current upheaval, Joyce wants to maintain some stability with a bank that she knows and used to trust.

Joyce has already set up an account with an English speaking Spanish bank, but Mike is unable to have his pension transferred to a bank outside the UK, which surprisingly is still the case with some pensions paid by a number of UK organisations; in this case a UK bank account is essential.

Clearly, the UK authorities have a problem with expats opening or maintaining a UK bank account, which is particularly strange when the customer is already known to the bank, as in Joyce and Mike's case. As well as having Spanish bank accounts, I was easily able to open a current account with a German bank a few months ago, so I fail to see why a British expat can no longer open or maintain a UK bank account from Spain, France or Italy.

The options for expats who wish to maintain or open a UK bank account have narrowed in the last two years or so and, to my knowledge, there are no longer any UK high street banks or building societies that are prepared to open new accounts for expats due to international banking legislation.

Hindsight is a wonderful thing, but it is clear that it is best for expats to be less than frank when dealing with a UK bank, and ask to use a relative's or friend's UK address for correspondence, or a mail redirection service that can offer a discreet address (further information about this on my Expat Survival page). Alternately, there is always the option of opening an offshore bank account, but I understand that these institutions require a more than substantial deposit, and are not that easy to pop into for a chat.

This issue is a worrying one, as experienced by expats living in Greece last year. Many expats were unable to access pensions paid into their Greek bank accounts during the height of the crisis, and the UK's Foreign and Commonwealth Office recommended that British expats open a bank account in the UK instead. It seems that this is no longer an option should similar circumstances arise again in Greece or another country. This could potentially become a more serious issue should the UK vote to leave the European Union, and expats are unable to meet current residency requirements for banking within a European member state, and wish to rely upon a UK bank.

If you have any personal experience of problems with your UK bank when leaving the UK, or difficulties in opening a UK bank account, please let me know for a future article. Specific information will, of course, remain confidential.

## Pineapple and Diamond Heists

A news item about the theft of 3000 pineapples from the neighbouring small island of El Hierro caught my eye this morning. The theft of such an important cash crop from an island that is by no means the most affluent of the Canary Islands will have been a devastating loss to the farmers concerned, and particularly since their insurance does not cover such losses. Since the theft took place after the crop had been harvested, packed and boxed, it is assumed that the fruit has already found its way for sale on the neighbouring islands and beyond.

All theft is wrong; someone gains at the expense of someone else, and can never be condoned. However, the circumstances of some thefts (or heists as Americans like to call it nowadays) are often amusing. The recent massive theft of fourteen million pounds worth of diamonds, gold and cash from a safe deposit facility in London's Hatton Garden was one example where I found myself laughing at the circumstances. Indeed, many a television journalist covering the story found it hard to keep a straight face when reporting certain aspects of this ingenious crime.

The thought of a group of elderly men, posing as gas engineers, led by a 76 year old who charmingly used his London Transport bus pass to get to the burglary, gives all elderly men and women considerable hope that they can get up to something rather more interesting that playing bridge or bowls all afternoon. The technical and physical skills of drilling though a thick concrete wall, without leaving a forensic trace, is little short of amazing for anyone, let alone the over 60s. Fortunately, no one was killed in this exploit, which would have dramatically changed public perception of this case.

This group of intrepid burglars used the Internet to research the equipment that they might need, equipped themselves with a diamond tester, diamond gauge, as well as a stock of informative magazines about diamonds. Despite nine million pounds worth of valuables being recovered, this crime will be remembered as the largest burglary in English legal history to date. At the time of writing, all but one of the gang members have been caught and prosecuted, and are now serving lengthy prison sentences.

Not only did the age and ingenuity of this plot gain these criminals considerable attention, as well as some admiration, they also thoughtfully provided a screenplay for a future film through the recordings made of their animated conversations in a London pub, as well as in a vehicle after the raid. I do hope that when a film is eventually made, which I am sure it will, the filmmakers consider asking Michael Caine to play one of the parts; he would be ideal.

Back to the theft of pineapples from the small island of El Hierro. Maybe the value of the pineapples was not as much as the diamonds from the Hatton Garden vaults, but I suspect that the loss of the fruit will be felt by farmers just as keenly as those who stashed their wealth in the Hatton Garden vaults.

## The Insurance Fraud

I was talking to a tour representative working in a large hotel in the Canary Islands recently. Over lunch, we touched upon the thorny subject of the behaviour of some British holidaymakers holidaying on the islands. I expected the discussion to refer to the over indulgence of alcohol and subsequent aggression, both in the resorts as well as on airlines bringing tourists from the UK. Instead, the subject turned towards fraudulent claims made by customers against tour operators.

It seems that an increasing number of holidaymakers are attempting to claim damages from tour companies and hotels on the basis of fraudulent claims of 'food poisoning' and such like. Indeed, a recent case of a couple from Northern England who appeared to have had a fault-free holiday on one of the islands, subsequently claimed for 'food poisoning' when they arrived home.

On the rare occasions, when such cases are genuine, most sick holidaymakers will immediately contact the hotel management for help, such as contacting a doctor for medical advice, or the whereabouts of the nearest chemist. Tour representatives are usually easily contactable and helpful in cases of medical emergencies. In this case, no contact was made to the hotel or the tour company, and no medical attention was sought in the resort. Upon their return to the UK, the couple immediately went to a solicitor and are currently attempting to sue the tour company for damages. In tandem with this action, the couple also went to the local press who, perhaps foolishly, took the couple at their word and wrote a full-page article condemning the tour company and the hotel.

Hopefully, the court will be able to see through such obvious fraud, and the couple will eventually be prosecuted. Sadly, behaviour such as this often has unintended consequences, creating a huge amount of damage to other people, including the wronged hotel and its staff, as well as the reputation of the tour company. In addition, this is one of the reasons why the insurance premiums of honest folk continue to rise.

Another current fraud is for holidaymakers to claim that they have been robbed of valuable possessions in their hotel or resort. Sadly, one of our friends was unwittingly drawn into a similar case of attempted fraud recently when trying to assist a holidaymaker who was in a state of distress outside a nightclub. He claimed that he had been mugged and relieved of his Rolex watch, valuable camera, top of the range mobile phone and a huge amount of cash; not exactly the kind of things that you would take with you when going to a nightclub that you have never been into before.

Our friend felt sorry for 'the victim' and helped him by taking him to the police station to report the crime in Spanish, as well as helping to complete police reports. Several hours later, the police discovered inconsistencies in 'the victim's' story, and 'the victim' was warned that wasting police time and making fraudulent claims are serious offences that could result in imprisonment. Sadly, our friend was also warned of serious consequences for aiding the individual, even though he had never met the man before and was only trying to assist a holidaymaker in trouble. In this case, 'the victim' was attempting to obtain a police report in order to claim for 'stolen items' from his insurance company; no doubt to pay for his next holiday.

# Consumer Rights in Spain

One of the advantages of buying products in Spain and the Canary Islands is that all goods that are sold come with a two-year manufacturers' guarantee, regardless of where the product is purchased. In addition, shops are obliged to accept the return of an unused item if you change your mind, within a fifteen-day cooling off period. This is one of the reasons why I, as an expat, much prefer to buy expensive items in Spain rather than from the UK, which offers a measly one-year guarantee. However, there are some annoying exceptions, for instance, some high value and high tech products, although sold with the obligatory two year guarantee, are exempted from product returns within the 15-day period if the seal on the box has been opened, unless the item is faulty.

In addition, manufacturers selling goods in Spain have to ensure that spare parts are available for at least six years following the date of sale. Although little known by the general public, this law is designed to discourage manufacturers from suddenly discontinuing the supply of replacement parts for major products at short notice, leaving purchasers with no option, but to purchase a more modern item. This form of planned obsolescence is, in theory, not allowed in Spain.

I have friends who were recently faced with this issue when an expensive coffee maker failed and required a replacement part. The replacement part was no longer available and, when challenged, the suppliers were forced to supply an equivalent replacement product free of charge, even though the coffee maker was over four years old. Many consumers are unaware of their rights in this matter.

This becomes more complicated with extended warranties, which provide cover for major appliances, such as washing machines and freezers, when the manufacturer's guarantee expires. There are insurance policies available for all major appliances from the better department stores, whilst some chains of electrical stores, as well as supermarkets selling electrical goods, offer purchasers the option to pay an additional fee to extend breakdown cover for a further 2 to 3 years. These add on deals often appear to be good value, or offered free, but as in most things in life, you get what you pay for, and some are hardly worth the paper that they are printed on.

In my own recent case, our three-year-old washing machine suffered a major breakdown. It was an expensive machine, bought from a well-known electrical store that I have used many times before on the basis that it would last longer than some of the cheaper models, and that I would have a reliable company behind the product. The manufacturer's two-year guarantee had expired and I therefore had to rely upon the additional warranty that I had purchased with the machine. I assumed that a telephone call to the store would bring a service engineer for the specific brand of washing machine to my home within a day or two. In reality, I had to wait for about a week before an engineer eventually appeared. The engineer was appointed by the store to repair and install a whole range of products, and was not a specialist engineer. The engineer took a quick look, shook his head, and told me that the machine was a "right off" and if repaired the part would be very expensive. Permission would have to be obtained from the insurance company before the repair could take place and he would have to write a report, sending a full quotation of costs to the store.

Four weeks later, there was no sign of either the machine being repaired or a replacement machine being delivered. Many phone calls to an expensive phone number and emails led to unhelpful customer service staff telling me to wait yet "another ten days" and eventually resulted in the same engineer returning to take away the machine for repair. It has now been four months since the washing machine broke down, and as yet there is no sign of a resolution or return of the washing machine, and in despair I have now bought a new one from another company. In addition, both the completion of the 'libro de reclamaciones' (complaints form), as well as reporting the issue to OMIC (the department responsible for consumer affairs at the Town Hall) has brought no resolution to the problem, so be very wary of the protection that these two so-called resolutions provide; I suspect that both approaches are little more than worthless bureaucracy.

Looking back, it would have been wiser to cover certain key appliances, such as washing machines, dishwashers and freezers, with a separate insurance policy through a named insurance company rather than through the add on deal offered at the till. This would have given me the option to request service and repair from the authorised dealer rather than a local generic agent who dabbles in the repair and installation of a whole range of products. The experience has failed to give me confidence in purchasing large items from this particular store again.

Generally, consumer protection in Spain is very good, but as in most things, we have to be careful, do our homework and accept that we usually get what we pay for.

**Update – Four months later**

A number of readers have contacted me since this article was published; it seems that I am not the only one to have this issue with company and their 'Guarantee Extra'.

From the time that the washing machine was collected from my home, with no notice of intended collection or receipt given, there was no contact from the company or the service engineer. Completion of the customer complaint form, as well as our insistence that the 'Guarantee Extra' should cover the repair brought no result.

In their defence, the company claimed that the repair was outside the cover of the guarantee, although we were not given a list of exceptions when the guarantee was purchased. In addition, we were given four different reasons about what was wrong with the machine.

We referred the claim to OMIC, the Town Hall body responsible for dealing with consumer disputes. They agreed to contact the company.

We heard nothing for four months, until one day we received a telephone call from OMIC to visit their office for a "resolution". This "resolution" was nothing more than a threat from the company that we either had to pay them for the repair of the machine, or they would make a charge to return the broken machine back to our home. In addition, if we didn't comply, the company would charge us one euro for each day that they stored the washing machine. OMIC didn't seem that interested in our protest, but said that they would respond to the company on our behalf.

We finally contacted the manufacturer of the washing machine, and they were very helpful. Even though the machine was well outside their guarantee, they agreed to intervene and speak to both the company and OMIC on our behalf. This they did, and reached agreement with the company to dispose of the machine, without cost to ourselves.

In conclusion, this was a worrying incident that did nothing to encourage us to shop with the company ever again. The customer complaint process, as well as the OMIC intervention, appeared to side more with the trader than the consumer. Without the intervention of the manufacturer of the washing machine, I suspect that this issue would have necessitated the intervention of a lawyer, which would have exceeded the cost of the washing machine. Finally, in most cases, 'Guarantee Extra' from this company should be avoided, as they may not be worth the paper that they are printed on.

## Between a Rock and a Hard Place

So, who has heard of the Savage Islands? I guess many have, if you happen to be Portuguese, but maybe less so if you happen to live elsewhere.

The Savage Islands are a small Portuguese archipelago in the North Atlantic, 280 kilometres south of Madeira, and close to the west coast of Africa. Sadly, despite the usual friendly relations between the two neighbours, there is now a growing dispute between Spain and Portugal. Basically, the argument boils down to the differences between an island and a rock, but is heavily influenced by endless greed for oil.

The archipelago is a Natural Reserve, and comprised of two major islands and several islets of varying sizes. The archipelago is administered by the Portuguese municipality of Funchal, Madeira, and is the southernmost point of Portugal. In 1971, the Savage Islands were designated as a natural reserve, recognising their role as a very important nesting point for several species of birds.

Portugal and Spain have been in dispute about the waters around the islands for many years, and in a proposal sent to the United Nations in 2014, Spain renewed its intention to demand a share of the potential prosperity in the waters off these islands. Portugal claims that the islands are islands, whereas Spain states that they are only rock formations, which makes all the difference under international law. A country has sovereignty over islands lying within 200 nautical miles of the coast, but this sovereignty does not exist with rocks. The status of the islands is also important for Portugal, since a decision will eventually determine Portugal's southernmost border.

Of course, once again, it is oil that is at the centre of the argument, since the area in question, which is broadly the size of Italy, contains a significant amount of oil and gas. Seizing an economic opportunity, the Spanish authorities filed an application with the United Nations to expand their continental shelf in the Atlantic between the Canary Islands and Madeira by 296,000 square kilometres.

Meanwhile, from mid-August 2016, Portugal's Maritime Police have started to patrol the disputed territory in order to "exercise state authority with regard to monitoring, surveillance and navigation safety, as well as supporting the protection and preservation of the marine environment, people and property". Police will also be based permanently on the Savage Islands, supported by the installation of radar, a water desalination plant and an energy supply system. However, by all accounts, the police are not too keen to be stationed on the island, since it is not permanently inhabited and which their union regards as "a decision that is offensive to human dignity". I would have thought an all-expenses paid holiday on a near-deserted island would be just the perk that many police officers would crave for. Mind you, with a name like 'The Savage Islands', maybe there is good reason for their reticence.

Of course, politics is, as usual, at issue here. Spain is expected to continue to raise the case of its dispute with the UK over the ownership of another 'rock',

Gibraltar. Since Spain feels so strongly about its territorial claims over Gibraltar, logically it should also respect Portugal's claim over the Savage Islands. Since both countries are members of the EU neither government wishes the dispute to get out of control, so maybe it will be kicked once again into the long grass. In any case, although Portugal and Spain will continue their verbal dispute, it is likely that the argument will eventually be resolved by mutual division of the disputed territory.

# Living and Working Abroad

## The 'Would-be' Expat

Several years ago, I launched a new website: http://thecanaryislander.com that was initially designed to support the tourism industry in the face of a looming recession. I soon began to receive emails from many would-be expats, and I began to include pages that related specifically to living and working in the Canary Islands and Spain, which also became the subject of several of my books.

The Canary Islander website continues to receive many visitors each week, and the most popular pages continue to be 'Living and Working in Spain and the Canary Islands'. I receive many emails from would-be expats asking for advice, and although I cannot answer all requests, I do try to include the content of many issues raised in my weekly 'Letters from the Atlantic'. One regular question is, of course, "How do I get a job in the Canary Islands?"

The lack of determination to fulfil their dream is often one of the things that surprises and disappoints me about many would-be expats. Many assume that there are jobs and accommodation waiting to be handed to them. I point out that, since these islands suffer from the worst unemployment in Europe, most jobs will usually be offered to the Canarians and Spanish who already live here and speak the language.

Requests for information about jobs offering full time contracts with health care and benefits also surprise me; has anyone seen one of these contracts recently? Others demand "at least the minimum wage", whatever that is nowadays. Suggestions that they may like to try a job in the catering or leisure industry where there is sometimes seasonal demand usually fall on deaf ears. One message this week states, "I am a nurse, and I am looking for a job in the hospital", followed by "I don't speak Spanish, but I could learn". Maybe a course in Spanish would be a good idea before applying for a job in Spain? Unrealistically, many of my correspondents are looking to find a job similar to the one that they have in the UK, offering similar pay and conditions, but with the added bonus of a life in the sun. Sadly, most will be disappointed, because many are unwilling to try something new and challenging, as well as creating an opportunity for themselves.

The harsh truth is that the good times for would-be expats are rapidly disappearing, and will change even more rapidly should the UK leave the European Union. Those halcyon years of free movement of people and jobs, together with affordable housing waiting for any expats wishing to move to a life in the sun in France, Spain, Portugal, Italy and Greece are coming to an end.

It is not all bad news, as opportunities do still exist for those would-be expats who are prepared to make an effort. Some of the most satisfied expats that I know are those that have created a job for themselves; they have spotted a demand and tried to fill it. I have neighbours and friends that work from home designing websites, logos or other computer-related tasks. Another has a market stall and does quite nicely selling candles, ornamental lights and other mood accessories to tourists. Another may be found in one of the commercial centres drawing cartoons of those who are prepared to take the risk. I know of a couple running a pet-sitting business, whilst another is a home hairdresser. These people will never be rich, but they are happy to be in a land of their choosing and earn enough to survive.

Of course, such work is not practical if the intending expat has a young family, health conditions, has expensive tastes or is not prepared to work hard. However, opportunities do and always will exist for the determined and those that do not expect to be simply handed an opportunity. Yes, it does take imagination, the ability to identify a need and the determination to succeed, but it can be done.

So for all those would-be expats who are expecting an opportunity to be handed to them on a plate, forget it. In today's world, it is unlikely to happen. Many commentators suggest that opportunities that currently exist, and which many expats have enjoyed over many years, will certainly reduce if the UK leaves the European Union. However, if would-be expats are determined enough to 'live their dream', they can make it happen.

## Having a Ball

One of my first introductions to expat life in Spain was a meeting with the then British Consul when I started working as a newspaper reporter in the Costa Blanca.

"Of course, the Brits come here to die," was one of the more profound statements fired at me, as I was furiously scribbling notes in my new reporter's notebook.

After this cursory introduction to the life of the expat, I began my daily routine of reporting about expats at work and at play. I met accountants who had become plumbers, plumbers who had become estate agents, as well as those who had no intention of ever working again, if they could help it.

Life was good, and at that time the pound-euro exchange rate meant that many expats who had sold their modest homes in the UK could live a life of relative luxury in the sun. For many, their days rapidly slipped into a booze-filled stupor, with life revolving around the many British bars that had been opened by established expats. Barbecues, eating outdoors, and late balmy nights enjoying a drink or two with friends were all possible. Despite this initial impression of a relaxed, carefree lifestyle, I soon found an undercurrent of activity and breathless excitement that I had never before experienced in the UK.

I found myself being invited to performances given by the members of a local tap dancing club. These elderly ladies attended a twice-weekly tap dancing class, with the eldest member being in her nineties. Many had never danced, let alone tap-danced before, yet performed with the agility and confidence of dancers several decades younger. Ballroom, ballet, as well as traditional Spanish dancing were all on offer too.

I met Brits, Germans and Scandinavians demonstrating a dedication to animal welfare that would melt the heart of the most hardened expat. Over time, their hard work proved to have a hugely positive impact upon attitudes to stray dogs and cats in the area. Walking groups, cycling, chess and stamp collecting clubs flourished, together with golf, bowls and that strange new addition to the sporting repertoire of the expat Brit, petanca. I found it hard to keep track of all the clubs and activities that were on offer.

It was as if a strange new liberation was taking place for the British retired expat. Gone were the endless hours of watching football on television, reading the tabloids and mowing the lawn, if the weather was reasonable, and replaced by a new carefree, outdoor lifestyle where most things are possible. What struck me most of all, was the health and rigour of so many elderly people. I met many who had been suffering from a variety of disabling physical conditions, as well as depression in the UK, who were suddenly mostly pain free, with many no longer on medication.

My mind returns to those first introductory comments from the British Consul some years ago. Maybe the

Brits do retire to Spain to die, but most are determined to have a ball before they go!

# A New Expat Life or an Extended Holiday?

A new survey of retired British expats has produced some interesting, but not surprising results. It claims that around one third of those interviewed intend to return to the UK, because they are dissatisfied with their expat experience, which includes increases in costs of living and financial concerns.

During my years as an expat living in Spain and the Canary Islands, I have come across people offering a whole range of reasons for moving to another country. For most, it is a healthy new life in the sun, which it isn't if one is determined to do little more that lie on a sunbed all day, drinking excessive alcohol, with one's skin turning to a similar colour and texture to that of a leathery hippopotamus.

For others, it used to be the advantageous pound - euro exchange rate; one could live happily on the proceeds of the sale a modest family UK home, and particularly when pensions stretched unbelievably far. The cava bubble has certainly burst on this one, and parity of the pound - euro rate, which happened a few years ago, may well happen again in the not too distant future, continuing to shatter many a dream of an easy life in the sun.

Despite rapid advances in personal communications, not surprisingly many expats miss family and friends who are still living in the UK, as well as 'British culture', feeling that they do not belong. Part of the reason for becoming an expat is to embrace a Spanish, French or Italian culture. Many expats cannot be bothered to do so, refuse to learn the language, to appreciate cultural traditions, or to mix with 'foreign' neighbours. Failure to integrate is the key to much expat unhappiness, as well as a desire to create 'Little Britain' at every opportunity. Needless to say, the locals tend get a bit fed up with what is seen as British arrogance. Sadly, the 'What's in it for me?' attitude is now far more prevalent than the experiences gained from learning about and fitting into a new community and culture.

The forthcoming EU referendum has opened wide the true reasons why so many expats are disenchanted about their expat experience, and many myths about the European Union are being rapidly invented. It is the threat to pensions and access to European health systems that is concentrating British expat minds wonderfully. Although I am fully in favour of remaining in the EU, and have always opposed the idea of referendums as a meaningless bureaucratic exercise designed by the 'political suits' to appease a generally unthinking and inarticulate electorate into believing that they have some sort of democratic control over their lives. In reality, of course, all it does is to create social and financial instability. Despite this, I am pleased that an opportunity has been created for expats to examine the true reasons behind their lives in the sun.

Negative comments regularly abound about what is perceived as 'Spanish and European bureaucracy', conveniently forgetting of course that Britain also has its fair share of pointless bureaucracy, which Spanish and French expats find equally confusing when living in Britain. Thankfully, expats are slowly realising that life is about to change, whether or not there is a vote to stay within the EU. This is probably a good thing, and maybe those who do not feel comfortable with life in Spain will head off 'home', leaving those of us who do enjoy life in this wonderful country to live in peace and harmony with our neighbours, as well as within the European family of nations.

It is so important that those setting out on the expat adventure do not simply regard it as an extended holiday and that they do their homework before setting off. There is still hope for the British expat, since the survey also found that younger expats, aged 25 to 35, are increasing and now make up 27 per cent of all British expats. As disenchanted expats finally head off back to Gatwick with their hopes and dreams of a new life in the sun shattered, hopefully the younger generation will adopt a more intelligent and enlightened approach to being a contented and fulfilled European expat.

## 'All Inclusive' Poverty

In a world where politicians continually remind us of the need for austerity in a bid to finally overcome the worldwide recession, we are becoming a society that is content to witness a growing demand for food banks, child poverty and the homeless on our streets. These issues are not confined to inner city London, San Francisco or Madrid, but are also an issue in the relatively wealthy Canary Islands, a holidaymaker's paradise - for some anyway.

Last week, my local supermarket once again generously participated in a drive to restock local food banks with much needed provisions. Shoppers were encouraged to give what dried and tinned food they could, which the supermarket matched in terms of additional stock. This is a welcome initiative and mostly very well supported by local people. It is ironic that these collections and food banks operate just a short distance away from the hotels that are serving enormous buffet breakfasts, lunches and dinners to their pampered guests. The food banks give a whole new meaning to the term 'all inclusive'.

'All inclusive' poverty is all around us and most of us see it every day. Each week, after I have filled my trolley in the local supermarket, I meet several men and women begging for cash. Usually, they want to take the empty trolley from me so that they can collect the one-euro deposit when it is returned. In recent months, I have noticed more people begging for money outside the doors of supermarkets on the island. Some are certainly chancers, whilst others appear to be genuinely in trouble. Many clearly have a serious problem with alcohol or drugs, whilst others appear to have made a career out of begging, with regular faces appearing each week. Most are friendly enough and accept refusals from shoppers, whilst I have seen others hurl verbal abuse at those who refuse to donate, and in one case I have seen anger spill into physical assault.

We are often told that we should not give cash to beggars on the streets, but to give regularly to specified charities instead. People tend to make one of three decisions when asked for their spare change. Some will look away; others will smile apologetically and say that they have no spare change, whilst others may give a coin or two. We are warned not to give to give to fraudulent people, as it encourages even more drunken behaviour and drug abuse, and some are not needy at all.

This is a problem that I have wrestled with for years. I am happy to give to someone in need, but how do I know that I am not making the matter worse? I remember once being stopped by an elderly woman who asked for some cash. I felt sorry for her, but refused to give her cash, since I suspected that she was an alcoholic. Instead, I told her that I would buy her a coffee and sandwich instead. She followed me a short way to the cafe bar, and then suddenly kicked me on the shins, picked up her skirts and fled as fast as her legs would carry her. She had clearly got the wrong message, and probably thought that I was trying to pick her up.

I have often thought that local charities for the homeless should set up a kind of 'Luncheon Voucher' scheme, whereby givers could buy books of vouchers from newsagents and local shops, and the vouchers could then be given to the needy on the streets, instead of cash. The vouchers could then be used in exchange only for hot drinks or food from participating shops and cafes. To my mind it would certainly make the difficult question of giving, and to whom we should give, much easier.

All-inclusive poverty must not become a norm that we are conditioned to accept. Not everyone who begs is a drug addict, alcoholic or a fraudster, and even if they are we must be careful not to lose sight of our common humanity.

## Still Trying to Watch Brit TV in the Sun?

Since I began writing for the expat community, the most frequent question that I am still asked is "How do I get Brit TV?" The same question is asked by expats everywhere, and much of it also comes with the frustrations that some expats feel when they have a UK TV licence, yet cannot legally receive a television service on holiday, or in their new home in the sun.

Over the last fifteen years or so, I have regularly reviewed a range of options ranging from strapping those awful baking tin arrangements to the highest point on the property, in order to receive retransmissions on a company's 'micro network', which basically meant capturing illegal retransmissions, to a fully fledged satellite system with a huge dish. If you were fortunate enough to get hold of a Sky card it worked rather well. However, once transmissions switched to another satellite, viewers in the Canary Islands, as well as many parts of Europe, suddenly found that they were once again without a signal, and the system was abandoned. There are now many abandoned satellite dishes on expat homes in the Canary Islands, Spain and much of Europe. It is a sad sight to see, but it did keep many British expat satellite installers employed for a number of years, so it wasn't all bad news.

Time has moved on, and with it faster Internet speeds for many, although sadly not all. We are now well into the era of the plug-in TV box, which does most of the hard work for you. It does, however, require a decent speed to prevent that dreadful 'buffering' that most expats are well aware of, an initial expense for the box and installation, as well as a monthly fee, which can be pricey once the 'introductory offers' come to an end. Most boxes work well to begin with, but the likely longevity of the company should also be taken into consideration, since many fail to stay in business for more than a few months. So, if readers do decide to go down this route, be prepared to take the risk and to lose some money in the process.

My personal recommendation is to get an Amazon Fire TV stick or Amazon Fire TV box, or the latest Apple TV box. The Amazon sticks and boxes are inexpensive - from about 25 pounds when I last checked. Although I am a steadfast fan of all things Apple, I am ashamed to admit that on this occasion, Amazon's offering is my preferred choice, as well as being much cheaper. You will also need a UK address, or a helpful relative or friends in the UK in order to purchase one of these gadgets from Amazon, since they will not post these overseas.

Once either of these units is plugged into your TV, setting up is straightforward. All you have to do is to download apps for the relevant TV network and you are almost ready to go. The key here is to get a DNS proxy; please note that this approach will not work unless you also have a DNS proxy set up on your modem. You can find out more about setting up a DNS proxy on the Expat Survival section of my website: expat.barriemahoney.com This approach may work by setting up with a VPN (Virtual Private Network), but I would not recommend it, as it restricts the speed and picture quality too much. This may seem complicated, but it isn't. Once it is set up, you can watch as much Brit TV as you wish.

Another advantage of this system is that once your Internet modem is set up with a DNS proxy, you can download the relevant apps on your smartphone or tablet and watch programmes wherever your Internet Wi-Fi signal stretches. You can also 'beam' programmes, pictures, music or videos from your smartphone or tablet to the Amazon or Apple TV boxes; you will probably be amazed at all the features that are opened up for you, and life as an expat may never be the same again!

Alternatively, you can just forget all about watching TV and head out to your balcony or patio with a good bottle of wine and a good book - which is so much more relaxing! After all, why did you really want to start a new life in the sun?

# Health Care for Expats in Spain – 'Convenio Especial'

Brexit continues to create anxiety for many expats planning to move to Spain and other European countries. One of the regular issues that people write to me about is health care, and particularly for those under state retirement age. Although I don't have any more information about what will happen to health care in Spain after Brexit, I am concerned that many expats moving to Spain are being coerced into purchasing private health insurance when there really is no need.

It is not unreasonable for Spain to ensure that newly arrived expats have the means to support themselves when living in the country, and this requirement includes health care. Indeed, evidence of a health insurance policy, as well as a number of other criteria are now sensibly required before newly arrived expats are given residential status. However, it appears that many banks are now using this requirement as an opportunity to sell expensive health cover to their clients, instead of advising them of the cheaper alternatives that are available. Expat websites, magazines, estate agents, lawyers and other information sources for expats are also guilty of pushing private health insurance, simply because they receive a hefty commission for each sign up. Even some furniture stores, that are popular with expats, are now interrogating their customers about their health care provision.

Whilst I have nothing against private health insurance, apart from clarity about premium increases and cover, as we get older, it is not the best option for everyone, and certainly not for those with existing medical conditions. My preference is to go with Spain's National Health Service that is, in most cases, excellent. On occasions, when we have required a second opinion or prompt, non-emergency treatment, I have to admit to using a private hospital, but that is always a second choice. I do, however, object to expats being coerced into a situation when they are led to believe that private health insurance is their only way of settling in the country.

As many readers will already be aware, despite various assurances, gifts and special offers when they take out a new health insurance policy, matters quickly change a few years later as they become older, and premiums are suddenly increased. In most cases, insurance companies know that we will pay up and shut up, simply because the older we get the more difficult it is to transfer to another, and possibly cheaper company. Some of the most worrying correspondence that I have received recently from expats relates to older expats who have found themselves priced out of the Spanish private insurance market as they reach the age of 70.

There is an alternative, and that is to purchase health cover from the Spanish health service. In most cases, following the age of retirement, most British expats of pension age will be entitled to free health cover anyway, so this issue will not be of concern to them. However, if you have retired early or do not qualify in the usual way, the following information may be useful.

Spanish regional health authorities offer a pay-in scheme for health care services. This is called 'Convenio Especial' and should be available from a local social security office. This is a public health care insurance scheme that is available throughout Spain to enable expats to access state-run health care. The scheme is managed by each autonomous region, so there may be some variations between them.

Most importantly, and unlike private health insurance, the scheme is offered regardless of pre-existing conditions. Children are already protected under Spanish law, as are pregnant women, and so there is no need to take out Convenio Especial for them, as they are entitled to free health care anyway. As far as I am aware, the only downsides are that if you wish to travel out of Spain, you do not have the right to claim a European Health card, and would need to take out private travel insurance for the period that you are away from home. In addition, expats are responsible for the full cost of prescriptions under this scheme. Do also be aware that patients are expected to have sufficient understanding of Spanish, since unlike most private hospitals, interpreters are not provided and it is a matter of luck whether or not your doctor or consultant speaks English.

Under the Convenio Especial scheme, expats pay a monthly fee of 60 euros per month for the under 65s, and 157 euros for those aged 65 and above, which compares very favourably with premiums charged by most private health insurance companies (not including special offers, or premiums merely designed to tempt you into signing up).

Some argue that those who can afford private health treatment should do so, since it puts less strain upon the National Health Service. Despite this, it is important for expats to have genuine and transparent choices when it comes to deciding upon important issues, such as health care. Much will depend upon affordability, but from my own limited research and contact with expats, it appears that many new expats are left unaware of Spain's NHS options that are available to them, and are instead being needlessly driven into the potentially exploitative arms of private health insurance companies.

# Living in Spain – The Paperchase

This is a subject that I am often asked about and, perhaps unsurprisingly, the number of requests has risen dramatically during the last few weeks following Brexit. Although this is a subject that I have written about on a number of occasions, I felt it was time for a refresh, since the rules and requirements rapidly change. Even so, intending expats should always check current information before committing themselves on the strength of this article. Also, please bear in mind that Spain is composed of autonomous regions, and so procedures may vary according to where you are applying.

**Requirements for Residency**

If you plan to live for more than 3 months in Spain, you must register with your local police station or foreigners' office (oficina de extranjeros). The application for residency will need to be completed in Spanish; however, you will find a copy of this document in English on my website, which you may find helpful. You will receive a residence certificate that states your NIE number (numero de identificacion extranjeros), which is a very important number that you will often need, as well as your name, address, nationality and date of registration. The original residence certificate has to last a long time, so you may wish to carefully protect it in a plastic cover.

A notario office or friendly police station can authenticate your photocopies with a legal stamp, for a fee, that many places accept instead of your actual residence certificate. However, for legal and town hall business, the original document is nearly always required.

You also need to show evidence that you can support yourself financially, as you will not be eligible to claim state benefits until you have worked in Spain with a contract for several years.

You will be asked to show that you have private health care insurance or that you have paid to join the Spanish National Health service if you are under the age of state retirement. Residents over the age of state retirement currently have full access to National Health services in Spain, although this may change if/when the UK leaves the European Union.

You will always need to show your passport when visiting police stations, foreigners' offices, tax offices and town halls, as well as your residence certificate. You will also be often asked for photocopies of your passport, and it is useful to have a supply of these. A notario office and police station can authorise your photocopies with a legal stamp that many places accept instead of your actual passport, but for legal and town hall business, the original will nearly always be required.

If you have a contract of employment with a Spanish company, you need to provide these details.

If you are self employed, you need to register at the local Social Security Office.

If you are not employed, then you need to prove you have other income or assets that you will use to live on, to avoid becoming a burden on the Spanish state; some regions may request that a specific amount of cash is readily available in your Spanish bank account. Your Spanish bank will provide information about your account and the money that you have deposited with them if you collect a form 790 from a local police station for a small charge.

As mentioned earlier, residency requirements can vary between the different regions of Spain, and you may often be asked to provide a padron certificate that you can collect from the local town hall. This padron (similar to the electoral roll) is important for the local town hall as it gives them information about how many people are living in the municipality, which can increase their funding. It is in your interests, as well as that of your municipality that you register at the town hall; registration will also give you the right to vote in municipal and European elections (whilst the UK is a member of the EU), but not national or regional elections.

Documents that are needed can be different across regions of Spain, so check with the police station or local town hall.

A certificate of residency is a very important document, and is needed for many day-to-day activities. Just one piece of further advice; if you do not speak reasonably fluent Spanish, you should use a gestor who speaks English to complete and register these forms for you. It can also save you many hours of waiting at the police station. If you do decide to do it yourself, prepare for a long day, take drinks, sandwiches and a comfortable picnic chair, as this is one piece of Spanish bureaucracy that I would try to avoid at all costs!

You can find a copy of the application form in English on my Expat Survival website: http://expat.barriemahoney.com

# Escape to the Ice

A few years ago, I wrote an article called 'Escape to the Sun', which was followed shortly afterwards by a book of the same title. Since that time, I am occasionally reminded by expats in other parts of the world that some expats are not particularly interested in the sun, but prefer to start a new life in cooler parts of the world. In order to address what some may see as an imbalance in 'Letters from the Atlantic', I offer the following story.

Older expats will remember those heady days after the Second World War, when the governments of both Australia and New Zealand encouraged a rapid growth in their population and prosperity by encouraging would-be British expats to relocate under their 'Assisted Passage' schemes. All it took was ten pounds per adult, with free passage for children, and a new life in a young and exciting country could begin. The governments of these countries promised housing, employment and generally a more optimistic future outside the UK. These expats become known as the 'Ten Pound Poms' and many of us will have family members or know of people who took advantage of this positive opportunity for migrants to seek a new life for themselves and their families. Later, there were similar government schemes on offer, with one engagingly called 'Bring Out a Briton'. These schemes reached a peak in 1969, but sadly ended in 1982.

The 'Ten Pound Poms' had an obligation to remain in the country for at least two years; otherwise they would have to refund the cost of their subsidised passage, which was substantial and therefore acted as a deterrent. Some returned home, but a large number failed to settle back in the UK, and returned to Australia and New Zealand once again. These expats became known as the 'Boomerang Poms'. Australia offered similar schemes to the Irish Republic, the Netherlands, Greece, Italy and West Germany, as well as Turkey, Malta and Cyprus. This was at a time when migration was seen as positive.

How things have changed; all this is in stark contrast to current world events where many view migrants in a negative and depressing light. The days of the 'Ten Pound Poms' are now long gone, or are they? In many ways, the free movement of people provided by the European Union has provided similar opportunities for expats to live and work in a country of their own choosing. Despite the uncertainties created by the Brexit vote, many continue to leave the UK to seek a better future for themselves and their families.

Now, getting back to the title of this 'Letter'; how about moving to Iceland? From what I hear, it is an incredibly beautiful country, with many friendly and welcoming people. Often known as 'The Land of Fire', Iceland has a great deal to offer the expat who is looking to escape from the UK and to start a new life in this Nordic nation. The crime rate is very low and murders are very rare in the country. Indeed, the World Economic Forum has voted Iceland as the most peaceful country in the world for the last six years.

If you are looking for happiness, Iceland came third in the table, just behind Denmark and Sweden for the happiness factor, according to the United Nations. There are mountains to explore, waterfalls to admire, as well as hot springs to soak in. It is also one of the best places in the world to admire and experience the wonder of the Northern Lights. What's not to like?

Iceland is currently rather keen to encourage British people who may be interested in locating permanently to their beautiful country. Following the world economic crisis, when Iceland was badly affected by its banking industry, its population fell rapidly as workers moved to other countries to find work. The time has now come to redress the balance and the country's economy is in need of a boost, which will be helped by an increase in migration to the country. One Icelandic budget airline is currently offering to refund the cost of the flight to Iceland if the traveller subsequently relocates to the country. All it takes is a signed lease agreement, employment confirmation, or university acceptance letter and a free flight and a world of new experiences could be yours.

All this sounds very appealing and I may visit Iceland one day. However, there is always a downside, isn't there? It is hard to overstate the importance of fish to the Icelandic people, since it remains the cornerstone of their economy. Over the centuries, fish has become a key source of the nation's food, as well as its wealth. Sadly, I really couldn't stay too long, since I have an aversion to the smell and taste of fish, which I gather the locals are rather keen on. Clearly, it takes all sorts.

## Getting Social

I received a message from Joyce and Henry this week, who are relatively new expats in Spain. They asked me for any advice that I could give them about getting to know people, as they were finding life quite lonely in their new home.

I know that some expats will disagree, but the fact is that for many expats in Spain, their social life exists around a purely bar and restaurant culture. Although this can be an acceptable way of making new friends for those who like bars, it can be a tedious waste of time for others. In smaller communities, such as the Canary Islands, where the choice of social activities is even more limited than Peninsular Spain, there are clear dangers in developing both a sedentary, if not alcoholic lifestyle, which are particularly unhealthy as we get older. On the darker side, we have lost a number of acquaintances in recent years through alcohol abuse, although the victims rarely accepted that they had a drink problem.

When we lived in the Costa Blanca, we found ourselves in virtually an all expat community. Whilst there were some downsides in not getting to know the real Spain, it offered considerable advantages in that we had a social network all up and ready to go. This was a huge advantage; we met many wonderful and interesting people, some of whom we are still regularly in contact with. 'Balcony Hopping' became the order of the day, as neighbours would spot us sitting on our balcony in the evening, and there was always an instant invitation to "join us for a drink". I shall never forget the kindness of so many people that helped us to settle easily into expat life.

Later, as we became more confident with the language and culture, we were ready to move to an all-Spanish community. However, for many expats, this can present a major problem. The Canarians, and indeed many Spanish, are totally family orientated and despite their courtesy and friendship on the surface, it is often difficult for many expats to make the friendships and relationships with their neighbours that they may be used to in the UK. This is, of course, one of the many reasons why expats gravitate towards communities representing their own nationality, which in turn leads to some criticism from our hosts that we are not 'joining in' and we are 'keeping ourselves to ourselves'.

So, back to Joyce and Henry; what are they to do? If a bar and restaurant social culture is not their thing, I usually suggest that newly arrived expats join group language study courses, which are sometimes offered by the local Town Hall. This is often a good way to meet other newly arrived expats who are trying hard to fit in. If newly arrived expats have a religious outlook on life, joining a local church will often offer a great deal in terms of community and friendship. Look out for music groups, walking groups, golf clubs, horse riding, chess clubs and flamenco dancing classes that are often offered by Town Halls too. Mixing with a range of nationalities, other than your own, can be challenging, but also great fun. Dancing and music crosses cultural boundaries, and can usually be an excellent strategy for breaking down initial apprehension and barriers.

When I worked as a newspaper reporter, I used to find that working as a volunteer for a charity was one of the best ways of getting to know other people. I fondly remember British, German and Swedish expats working amazingly well together to rescue and rehome stray dogs and cats. Compassion and the desperate need to do something to improve the plight of many of these poor, unloved creatures did much to unite and create a bond of friendship between expats from a variety of nations.

In today's turbulent times, with many migrants landing on our shores in desperate need of shelter and support, I know of many expats doing their best to assist them. Helping with translation, caring for children and accompanying migrants to Town Halls, health centres and other official bodies are just some of ways in which expats can help others, as well as beginning to create a social network for themselves.

In short, I guess what I am saying, is that in the very act of 'putting something back', we are creating a new life and social experiences for ourselves. So, to Joyce and Henry, off you go!

# Back to School - a reflection

It is that time of the year again. It is a time when the streets, playgrounds, shopping centres and cafe bars on the island fall silent (well, almost!), and once again it is possible to obtain some kind of service from the Town Hall, banks and offices as staff, somewhat grudgingly, return to work after nearly two months of disruption. The children are safely back in school and everyday life returns more or less to normal, until interrupted by the occasional fiesta and the next major holiday season. School holidays in Spain seem to go on for ever, and by the time that September comes, many parents have reverted from the often heard delusionary comment that "It will be good to spend some time with the kids again", to "Thank goodness, they are back in school". Most parents are hugely relieved, and I know that many children are happy to have routine and structure back in their lives again too.

As with all teachers, my year used to begin in September, with planning and preparation playing a large part of the long summer holidays that teachers and the education system are often criticised for. It was always a time to recover, both physically and mentally, from the rigours of the previous academic year, but it was also a time when colds and flu set in for a week or two. It was if the body knew that it could now take a break, since school was closed, which allowed all manner of disease to take hold and annoyingly interfere with holiday plans. In June this year, I recall seeing a Canarian neighbour and teacher, returning wearily from school during those last frantic days of the summer term, laden with a heavy bags of books, boxes and carrier bags. The weary smile and the sigh said it all, and I remember that feeling of exhaustion only too well.

I enjoyed teaching, and if I had my time over again I would choose exactly the same career. I recall starting each term with 35 or so anxious faces in their new classroom, dressed in new or freshly laundered uniforms, looking at me and wondering how it would all turn out. In turn, I recall thinking how small and unsure they all looked, and doubting that they would ever turn out as good a class as I had taught the previous year. I was always wrong, and when the end of term came the following July, I remember how much I missed them; all the individual personalities and potential, and the discoveries and learning that we had all achieved together. These were special and exhilarating times; exhausting, but nevertheless very special.

A few days ago, a friend asked me if I missed going back to school in September. My response was "Certainly not!" However, when I take time to reflect, I guess I do miss the routine of setting up a new classroom, the smell of fresh polish on the floors, repainted classroom walls and maybe new carpeting or a new piece of equipment if the budget allowed. I miss the fresh displays on classroom walls designed to welcome, entertain and intrigue new and anxious pupils, filling in a new class register, trying to remember new names, identifying the personalities that would challenge, entertain and infuriate me in the weeks and months ahead. I miss welcoming new colleagues and reassuring anxious parents.

I then have a reality check, and remember endless, and often pointless meetings, with school governors who would often take hours reaching a decision that myself and my staff could usually make in minutes. I recall helpful, supportive governors too who did their best for their school and their local community, as well as those 'local worthies' who were only there because of their position, and also those who were only interested in matters that would benefit their own child rather than the wider community.

I remember school parent teacher associations, sometimes called Friends' Associations, which were often a nightmare of the worst kind. In theory, most support schools well, but could often deteriorate into a kind of second governing body, not content with fund raising and supporting the best endeavours of the school, but challenging and arguing against school policies and decisions, and particularly those issues affecting their own child and not the wider community. I remember hours of meetings, fund raising and social events. Many were a privilege to participate in, whilst others I prefer to forget.

A few years ago, a friend who was also a head teacher on the island at the time, kindly offered me a teaching job. It took me all of five seconds to think about it and decline her kind offer. I believe that one of the important things in life is to recognise our own sell-by dates, and to be prepared to move on. This strategy applies not only to jobs, but also maybe to where we live, relationships, routines and the way that we live our lives. We need to continually re-evaluate our purpose in life and where we fit into the big plan. Life is short, and we need to make the most of all the opportunities that come our way.

So, at the beginning of this new academic year, I wish all our youngsters and their teachers well. Learn well together, and make the most of your potential. As for me, I have many happy memories, but relieved that I am no longer part of it.